Cambridge Elements

Elements in Middle East Politics
edited by
David B. Roberts
King's College London
Louise Fawcett
University of Oxford
Mohammed Abdel-Haq
King's College London

WHAT IS THE MIDDLE EAST?

The Theory and Practice of Regions

Marc Lynch
The George Washington University

CAMBRIDGE
UNIVERSITY PRESS

Shaftesbury Road, Cambridge CB2 8EA, United Kingdom

One Liberty Plaza, 20th Floor, New York, NY 10006, USA

477 Williamstown Road, Port Melbourne, VIC 3207, Australia

314–321, 3rd Floor, Plot 3, Splendor Forum, Jasola District Centre, New Delhi – 110025, India

103 Penang Road, #05–06/07, Visioncrest Commercial, Singapore 238467

Cambridge University Press is part of Cambridge University Press & Assessment, a department of the University of Cambridge.

We share the University's mission to contribute to society through the pursuit of education, learning and research at the highest international levels of excellence.

www.cambridge.org
Information on this title: www.cambridge.org/9781009557887

DOI: 10.1017/9781009557870

First published 2025

A catalogue record for this publication is available from the British Library

ISBN 978-1-009-55788-7 Hardback
ISBN 978-1-009-55789-4 Paperback
ISSN 2754-7817 (online)
ISSN 2754-7809 (print)

What Is the Middle East?

The Theory and Practice of Regions

Elements in Middle East Politics

DOI: 10.1017/9781009557870
First published online: February 2025

Marc Lynch
The George Washington University
Author for correspondence: Marc Lynch, marclynchgwu@gmail.com

Abstract: The Middle East has traditionally been understood as a world region by policy, political science, and the public. Its borders are highly ambiguous, however, and rarely explicitly justified or theorized. This Element examines how the current conception of the Middle East emerged from colonialism and the Cold War, placing it within both global politics and trends within American higher education. It demonstrates the strategic stakes of different possible definitions of the Middle East, as well as the internal political struggles to define and shape the identity of the region. It shows how unexamined assumptions about the region as a coherent and unified entity have distorted political science research by arbitrarily limiting the comparative universe of cases and foreclosing underlying politics. It argues for expanding our concept of the Middle East to better incorporate transregional connections within a broader appeal for comparative area studies.

Keywords: Middle East, regionalism, area studies, region, international relations

ISBNs: 9781009557887 (HB), 9781009557894 (PB), 9781009557870 (OC)
ISSNs: 2754-7817 (online), 2754-7809 (print)

Contents

1 Introduction: Is the Middle East a Region?

For much of the last fifteen years, I have directed the Middle East Studies M.A. Program at George Washington University's Elliott School of International Affairs. Like most of our peers, our program encompasses the Arab world, Iran, Turkey, and Israel. But almost every year, at least one student would want to focus on Afghanistan – fair enough, given America's two decades of war there. I would have to tell them that Afghanistan fell under the rubric of the Asian Studies Program. But, despite the presence of an outstanding historian of Afghanistan on the faculty, the truth is that Afghanistan was an unwelcome stepchild there as well, in a program which had to cover the languages, politics, and economies of a vast region sprawling from China to Japan, East Asia to Southeast Asia, and even India.

But even if Asian Studies could handle Afghanistan, the answer would still be unsatisfying. Afghanistan, after all, hosted al-Qaeda at the time it planned and executed the 9/11/2001 attacks on America which ignited the Global War on Terror and so much more. Al-Qaeda itself was the offspring of officially tolerated Saudi Salafist activism, failed Egyptian jihadist insurgency, and the ugly aftermath of the Saudi-US-backed Mujahideen insurgency against Soviet occupation. The US invasion of Afghanistan in 2001 paved the way for the 2003 invasion of Iraq, as well as the consolidation of America's imperium across what was briefly called the Broader Middle East. As the Afghan war bogged down into nearly two decades of frustrating counter-insurgency, much of the campaign was coordinated and implemented from an American airbase in Qatar. In other words, little of the military and strategic history of the "Middle East" after 2001 could really be told without at least some reference to Afghanistan. And yet it remained stubbornly outside the remit of Middle East Studies institutions or expertise.

The exclusion of Afghanistan from the Middle East was only one of many puzzles and frustrations which I encountered as my research interests and professional programming evolved. A pivotal moment came from a workshop which I organized along with my colleagues Zachariah Mampilly and Hisham Aidi at Columbia University in February 2020, just before the COVID shutdowns began. The workshop focused on transregional connections and comparisons between Africa and the Middle East. It zeroed in on the historical processes by which regions had taken on a sort of ontological reality despite very little basis in objective reality. The Horn of Africa, for instance, is separated from the Arabian Peninsula by little more than an easily traversable – and long traversed – body of water; Oman once ruled Zanzibar, and Swahili remains an official language across the Gulf littoral states. The Sahara Desert may be a formidable physical landscape separating the North African coast from the rest of the continent, but it hardly blocked transit and trade; the historical connections between the Maghreb and the Sahel run deep, despite the best efforts of French colonialism to divide them. Meanwhile, Middle East scholars often told the story of the late Ottoman Empire in ways focused so tightly on the Great Arab Revolt and the rise of pan-Arabism that they ignored parallel processes across the European provinces of the Empire as well as the deep connections between the Arab provinces and British India, which often directly governed them.

In short, conventional maps of the "Middle East" increasingly seemed to me more of a barrier to understanding than an asset. That is not to discount the importance of local expertise and area knowledge, of course. Good scholarship on the countries and peoples of the region certainly required mastery of local languages, extended field research, and all the other conventional markers of area studies. But at the same time, I found it harder and harder to understand why certain countries were deemed comparable and others were not. Why should we understand all Arab countries as somehow comparable despite their very different colonial histories, economic characteristics, political systems, and local cultures? Why compare political mobilization in Yemen, Egypt, and Tunisia while ignoring contemporaneous protests in East or West Africa? Is the Middle East really particularly war-prone when compared with, say, Central Africa or the Balkans? Does oil in the Middle East somehow matter differently than it does in Nigeria, Venezuela, or the United States? And, more broadly, what are the political and normative implications of dividing the countries of the Middle East from the broader Global South, implicitly or explicitly rendering their politics and aspirations as somehow unique?

My misgivings, I came to discover, were shared increasingly widely across many different area studies fields, and had been for a long time. The 2013 relaunch of the Duke University Press journal *Comparative Studies of South Asia, Africa and the Middle East*, for instance laid out an explicitly transregional approach and sought "to bring the study of region into sustained conversation with the humanistic and social science disciplines" (even as its title implicitly continued to reify the regions in question) (Mission Statement 2013). The turn to Oceanic Studies – and Indian Ocean Studies in particular – increasingly integrated the Arabian Peninsula into the South Asian and East African areas to which its coastal areas had historically belonged. These trends were encouraged first by the 1990s trend of globalization and internationalization studies, and then in the 2000s by policy interest in the global war on terror. Studies of migration in the 2010s on the one hand, and of jihadist insurgencies on the other, increasingly forced both scholarship and policy to break down the long-standing walls between North Africa and the Sahel and between the Gulf and South Asia. When I published "The End of the Middle East" in *Foreign Affairs* in 2022, I anticipated considerable pushback, or at least, sullen disinterest; instead, it became one of the most widely read articles of the year and generated a tremendous amount of productive discussion across both academic and policy discourse communities.

As I began to explore these ideas, I discovered very similar reflections and doubts across the other area studies. A 1997 special section of *Africa Today* explored the crisis of the area studies from an African perspective, responding to changes at the Social Science Research Council which prioritized global issues over regional studies. Southeast Asianists similarly asked the value of a regional concept which included dozens of highly diverse countries, often separated by oceans and sharing little by way of religion, language, or shared historical experience. Latin Americanists argued with the colonialist implications of a region defined by the European languages of their colonizers. Africanists asked what besides skin color made all of sub-Saharan Africa a region. The dialogues within these other regions, and the intellectual progress they stimulated, looked somewhat different from what I knew from the Middle East, though. South Asian Studies pioneered subaltern studies, Latin Americanists developed dependency theory, and Africanists developed original and influential theories of the warscape. While all of the area studies grappled with the colonial origins of knowledge production and the legacies of imperialism, and all eventually rebelled against the marginalization of scholars from the regions within the ranks of the academy, the different trajectories of the arguments intrigued me. I learned as much from the other area studies when researching this Element as I did from my colleagues within Middle East Studies.

There has been a long history of reflections on the concept of the Middle East, sprinkled across disciplines and journals, which informs the arguments in this Element (Bonine, Amanat, and Gasper 2012). Questioning the definition of our region, it turns out, is almost as hardy a perennial ritual of passage for Middle East Studies as is decrying its ostensible failures (Lynch, Schwedler, and Yom 2022). Those critical perspectives, from some of our most influential scholars across multiple fields – Nikki Keddie, Jerrold Green, Rashid Khalidi, Charles Kurtzman, Nile Green, Asef Bayat – share a remarkable consistency. Almost all point out the absence of linguistic, ethnic, cultural, or historical foundations for the grouping of states, the geopolitical origins of the concept (usually with reference to Admiral Mahan and the rise of American naval power), and almost all ultimately conclude with a pragmatic acceptance of the regional definition in order to get on with things. I agree with and build upon those past examinations, but hope to do something more. In this Element, I argue for taking the contested definition of the region as itself an important topic of inquiry, dig deep into the costs and benefits for both policy and theory of particular definitions of the region, and suggest how different definitions of the region become useful for specific research questions and political projects rather than more or less closely approximating some objective truth.

The matter seems far from settled. For all the questions about the reality of the Middle East as a region, the Arab uprisings of 2011 revealed a region very much in and of itself, one where membership in the region did indeed demarcate unique political dynamics. Protest diffused far more within the Arab portions of the region than beyond it, interventions were more likely inside the region than outside of it, the media covered events inside the region differently from outside of it, and Arabs identified far more with what happened within the region than outside of it (Lynch 2012). The escalating military role of Iran, Turkey, and Israel within the region in the following years brought strategic life to their inclusion in the region, despite their exclusion by way of identity politics and protest diffusion (Lynch 2016). Indeed, the Middle East was arguably never more of a region than in the dizzying years after 2011, as the UAE, Qatar, and Saudi Arabia intervened more directly and intensely in the Arab world than ever before. At the same time, those states globalized toward Asia and international institutions more intensely than ever before, from the intense competition among Arab states, Turkey and Iran for a foothold in the Horn of Africa and Libya to Turkish–Iranian competition in the Caucasus to the spread of Islamist insurgency from North Africa to the Sahel.

This Element therefore examines the concept of the Middle East as a region for the purposes of political science analysis. It begins (Section 1) by showing how the Middle East has been defined, operationalized, and theorized within political science; how it was institutionalized within universities and think tanks for specific purposes of knowledge production; and how those approaches have been critiqued from within and outside political science. It then (Section 2) explores the construction of the Middle East as region through geopolitical competition and external impositions of order. Rather than stop there, however, it then (Section 3) shows how the Middle East as region has structured the political playing field for generations of political actors and movements, including pan-Arabists, Islamists, and non-Arab powers such as Israel, Turkey, and Iran. Then (Section 4) it returns to political science and demonstrates the costs and benefits for academic work of adopting particular definitions of region, showing the distortions and limitations introduced by assumptions of comparability and artificial shortening of the universe of cases. It concludes (Section 5) with reflections on the broader implications of thinking and practicing regions.

When presenting the ideas for this volume, I have routinely been asked at the end what the Middle East actually is, then. After all the problematizing and the questions, which states ultimately should be included in the Middle East? This, I believe, is ultimately the wrong question. Different definitions will be useful for different purposes, and ultimately the question being asked should determine the appropriate universe of cases. The traditional definition of the Middle East may make good sense for a study of the diplomatic history of the Cold War, but be completely inappropriate for a study of Islamist political movements. The Element ultimately argues for taking the fluidity and contested nature of Middle East as a core question for both theory and practice, and advocates for thinking transregionally and cross-regionally when formulating questions, research designs, and policy recommendations.

2 What Is the Middle East?

What is the Middle East, and why does defining it matter for political science? Most people have a general sense of what countries are part of the Middle East, informed by journalistic practice and what seems like a geographical common sense: the Arab countries, Israel, Iran, and Turkey. Further, most would likely agree on first glance that those countries make up a region which has distinctive and unique qualities: perhaps more violent than other regions, or more religious, or more autocratic. Those assumptions are generally pre-theoretical, if not atheoretical, however. The Middle East's boundaries are, in fact, among the least obvious and most contested of almost any world region. They are politically constructed, as are all regions, and regularly politically contested in ways that belie their seeming self-evidence. The obvious borders and nature of the region begin to look a bit fuzzier when one considers the historical and growing connections between the Arabian Peninsula and the Horn of Africa, the economic and security porosity of the Sahara Desert separating North Africa from its southern neighbors, or the activity of Iran and Turkey across both central Asia and Africa. The ostensible linguistic unity of even the Arab portions of the region collapses on first contact between a Gulf Arab and a Moroccan, as witnessed during the 2022 World Cup in Qatar, when Arabic broadcasters proved unable to interview the stars of the Moroccan squad in Arabic.

At the most basic level, defining the Middle East matters because political scientists and policymakers act as if it exists. They shape their analysis, design their research, enact policies, and craft recommendations based on the often unexamined assumption that there is such a thing called the Middle East which has distinctive characteristics. The assumption that the Middle East is a world region underlies the organization of the US foreign policy apparatus (and that of most other states), the institutions of knowledge production and higher education, a wide range of scholarly and policy oriented research and publications, and popular discourse. The division of the world into identifiable regions – Africa, Asia, Europe, Latin America, the Middle East, South Asia – is taken for granted in everything from the popular board game _Risk_ to the selection of members on the United Nations Security Council. It is telling that a major review of Middle East Studies based on a ten-year, multi-foundation supported project which is otherwise a model of critical inquiry does not at any point problematize the definition of the Middle East (Shami and Idriss-Miller 2016). For much of IR theory, the Middle East could usefully be treated as "a region like any other" – a self-enclosed geographic entity governed by an identifiable regional order (Valbjørn 2003; Teti 2007).

The utility of the regional concept has been questioned, poked, and prodded by political scientists almost from the moment of their creation in their current form in the years following World War II. Scholars and policymakers routinely acknowledged the artificiality of these regional constructs, noting the internal diversity of the ostensibly distinctive regions, the porosity of their boundaries, and the risks of treating them as homogenous blocs. Of the regions, the Middle East and Southeast Asia were often recognized as the least likely natural units, not covering a single continent or peninsula (like Africa, Latin America, and South Asia) and lacking common political institutions (like Europe and the then-Soviet Bloc). Still, trends within international relations and political science, reinforced by government and foundation funding patterns and the exigencies of the Cold War, reinforced region-thinking in ways that resonated with distinctive historical and intellectual trends surrounding Middle Eastern history. Ahram (2011: 70), in an appeal for comparative regional analysis, argues that "rather than geographic givens, regions are analytic categories grounded in historical processes that cluster spatial, temporal, and institutional contexts between and above the country-level unit." Börzel and Risse (2016: 7), in their authoritative handbook of comparative regionalism, "define regions as social constructions that make references to territorial location and to geographical or normative contiguity." But what does that mean, specifically, for the Middle East?

This section begins with general approaches to region and regionalism within political science and the relationship between region and US foreign policy interests, and then turns to the Middle East as a particularly fraught example of such world regions. Throughout, I emphasize both the particularity of the Middle Eastern experience and the remarkable similarities it shares with the experience of the other regional area studies in the post–World War II academy. As with many other regions, there is no clearly objective referent for the Middle East as a region and considerable ambiguity about its geographic boundaries. At the global and strategic levels, certain parts of the grouping of regional states make some sense (see Section 3), while other groupings make sense at the normative and identity levels (see Section 4). Both dimensions need to be taken seriously for the purposes of political science (see Section 5). Here, we place the evolution of the regional construct in the American academy and within key strands of International Relations theory before turning to critical approaches.

Regions in IR Theory

Regions and regionalism were central to the foundation of post–World War II IR theory and political science. A robust literature examined the emergent European experiment with integration, and from the start speculated about the possibilities of replicating that liberal institutionalist design in other world regions. IR theorists in the 1950s and 1960s routinely examined regions as subunits of the global order, conceptualizing regions such as the Middle East as "subordinate international systems" (Binder 1958), "regional international politics" (Thompson 1973) and "regional subsystems" (Cantori and Spiegel 1969; 1973). Comparing these subordinate regional systems was a growth industry, meriting, for instance, an *International Studies Quarterly* special issue in 1973. Cantori and Spiegel (1973) described regions in terms of a core, a periphery, and an intrusive system (i.e. external powers) in ways quite similar to Buzan and Waever's later explication of regional security complexes, fleshing out those conceptions with a set of "pattern variables" (the balance of power, the nature of communications, the nature and degree of cohesion, and the structure of relations). The regional substructure of international relations was largely taken for granted as the medium through which Cold War bipolarity flowed, with area studies charged with explaining the particularities of regional experience as part of a broader international contest for influence, power, and security. The study of regions, as Thompson (1973) observed decades before the area studies controversy rocked political science, presented "an opportunity for the integration of the findings of area specialists and international relations students."

Even as the literature on region developed, however, it remained something of a truism that "regions" represent an amorphous category which typically fails to capture any sort of objective reality about the lived experience, political dynamics, or security concerns of those who live within them. Russett (1967) proposed that regions should be defined by "geographic proximity, social and cultural homogeneity, shared political attitudes and political institutions, and economic interdependence." But the degrees of such shared characteristics and the blurring of the boundaries always caused analytical confusion. Thompson (1973) compared more than two dozen studies of Middle Eastern international relations and showed the remarkably low overlap in the countries included. Decades of scholarship critiqued the concept of region by pointing to the absence of objectively measurable commonalities which would make for analytical coherence. Latin America may be largely Catholic and Spanish-speaking, but Brazil – one of its largest powers – is not. Asia speaks dozens – indeed, hundreds – of languages, and contains countries ranging from the vast land terrain of China to the archipelago of islands of Indonesia. Even the most straightforward territorial demarcation of region based on continental scale is more problematic than it appears; it is not obvious, as Ali Mazrui (1974) pointed out decades ago, why the narrow breadth of the Red Sea divides Africa from Arabia while hundreds of miles of the Sahara Desert do not divide the African continent.

All of this is today largely forgotten. Regional analysis faded from fashion in the 1980s, with most of the publications on regional subsystems from that era disappearing from view so thoroughly that today they are virtually never cited or included on even the most comprehensive syllabi devoted to the IR of the Middle East. The rise of Waltzian style neorealism pushed scholars to look for universal patterns derived from the structure of the system and to abstract away from regional or local particularities. With Realists arguing that patterns of balancing and bandwagoning could be explained through rigidly parsimonious calculations of power under anarchy, the value of regional expertise came to be devalued. That aligned well with the rational choice and formalizing trends within the rest of political science, all of which prioritized the search for universalizable rules of politics and downgraded area knowledge. When constructivism rose to challenge the dominance of Realism in the 1990s, it tended to take regions at face value in order to examine how regional norms or institutions might lead to systematic deviations from Realist expectations (Barnett 1998; Lynch 1999). The diminished focus on regions coincided with the broader crisis of the area studies in the 1990s (see further), where key foundations such as the SSRC dismantled the institutional architecture of funding and support to the area studies in favor of a focus on globalization and transnational trends.

The 1990s and 2000s, surprisingly, proved to be a boom time for the study of regions in international relations (Börzel and Risse 2016). The newfound interest in regions derived in part from the perceived success of the European Union, but also from the empirical rise of regional organizations across many of the world's regions which sought to emulate the EU model, the increasingly autonomous dynamics of regions freed from the Cold War's confining structures, and the general rise of constructivism within IR theory. The "new regionalism" responded to the processes of globalization and looked at the multiscalar forms of regional adaptation (Hettne 2015). Much of the interest in the so-called "new regionalism" in IR theory revolved around questions of comparative regionalism and regionalization, driven in large part by the empirical growth of regional economic cooperation and the development of attendant formal organizations, and often approaching the problem through the lens of neoliberal institutionalism and economistic rather than culturalist assumptions (Mansfield and Solingen 2010). The intellectual agenda focused on the relative institutionalization of regional organizations, often with the European Union as an explicit or implicit touchstone for comparison. The appeal of the European model for comparative regionalism is clear. After World War II, the states of Europe managed to overcome centuries of destructive warfare through the creation of supranational organizations and the opening of borders to trade and mobility. The transformative effects of the European Community, and then the European Union, on every level from security, law, and economies to culture and norms offered one of the most powerful examples of structural change and construction of liberal order in the history of world politics.

Regionalism studies typically sidestepped the definitional questions about regions by focusing on the organizations – ASEAN, the African Union, Mercosur – and evaluating their progress (usually deficient) toward matching this great European transformation (Fawcett and Gandois 2010; Valbjørn 2016). It is small surprise that the Middle East was largely absent from a literature with such a focus, despite the power of pan-Arabism as an ideological movement and the material underpinnings of regional connectivity (among the Arab countries, at least). The Middle East stands out for the absence of regional organizations, political, or economic regional arrangements and any of the kind of formal regionalism prioritized in such studies (Aarts 1999; Fawcett and Gandois 2010; Legrenzi and Calculli 2013). The Arab League includes only the Arab parts of the region, and is remarkably nonfunctional by any standard (as opposed to the GCC, which for decades developed into a functional institution at the subregional level). Despite the best of American efforts to create regional institutions which included Israel – or Iranian and Turkish attempts to gain access to such institutions – no fully and exclusively Middle Eastern regional organization exists (efforts such as the Baghdad Pact in the 1950s resulted in explosive regime-threatening popular protests across the region). Where the Middle East figured in such studies, it was usually only by noting the absence of whatever features were deemed necessary for liberal order building: democracy, economic integration, supranational organizations, a globalizing middle class, and so forth. While comparative regionalism made tremendous strides as a research program (Börzal and Risse 2016), much of the intensive comparative work on institutional design, economic outcomes, and legal layering simply has little relevance to the Middle East.

The Middle East, or at least the Arab parts of it, fits more comfortably in the study of pan-regionalism than in the study of regionalism in the sense of formal institutions. Comparisons to pan-Africanism and pan-Asianism, focused more on societal level identification and expectations than on intragovernmental cooperation or international institutions, briefly put pan-Arabism at the center of comparative regionalism. Nasser's pan-Arabism drove politics across the region, building shared identity through political practice from the Gulf to the Levant. The dispersal of Palestinians after 1948, and of Muslim Brothers from Egypt after 1952, and the broader flow of Arab workers into the Gulf, provided material foundations for regional integration.

But that attention faded along with those pan-regional political movements. Pan-Arabism and pan-Africanism may have seemed like urgent objects of study in the 1950s, but by the 1980s those movements had been tamed, discredited, and abandoned. At the same time, methodological preferences in political science strongly tipped interest toward the more concrete and measurable study of the creation and effects of institutions and away from the more amorphous traffic in ideas and identities. The constructivist turn in IR theory of the 1990s did lead to something of a revival of interest in pan-regionalist movements and the cultural dimensions of regionalism. Barnett (1998) developed an influential conceptualization of Arab regional order built around symbolic competition over norms of regional order which took the region as the unit of analysis. Lynch (2007) explored the rise of satellite television and the internet as foundations of a regionwide Arab public sphere, uniting at least the Arab portion of the region politically through discourse and a synchronous shared experience familiar to readers of Benedict Anderson. It was only with the 2011 Arab uprisings, however, that approaches based on a regional public sphere fully consolidated.

More security-centric and structural approaches to regions and international order have also paid attention to the Middle East as a region. Buzan and Waever's influential *Regions and Powers* (2003) takes the Middle East as one of its core case studies. It takes as the starting point for regional security complex theory that "since most threats travel more easily over short distances than long ones, security interdependence is usually patterned into regionally-based clusters" (Buzan and Waever 2003: 3). This geographic conception of region runs into a multitude of empirical and conceptual problems, of course, many of which will be detailed later in this section. Regional Security Complexes are ultimately defined as "durable patterns of amity and enmity taking the form of subglobal, geographically coherent patterns of security interdependence." They explicitly reject the idea of defining regions in terms of whether those in the region identify with it (they assert that the Middle East is a region, even though its people do not recognize it) (Buzan and Waever 2003: 48); what matters is their security practices, and whether they behave as if they are part of a shared security region. What makes the region, then, is its wars and the security interdependencies that result.

Katzenstein's *A World of Regions* takes a similarly eclectic approach as it attempts to situate the Middle East within American imperium. His conception of regions is that they are porous, and include both material and symbolic dimensions which are ultimately observed in political practice. In his historical account, the borders and purpose of both Europe and Asia were as contentious and fluid as they are in the Middle East. His primary focus is Asia and Europe, where he sees core states linked to the United States ordering regional politics. The Middle East, joined by Africa, Latin America, and South Asia, lacks such an intermediary. It is provocative, and somewhat disturbing, to consider his suggestion that Washington perhaps conceived of the invasion and occupation of Iraq in order to transform it into such a pro-American core state, in the model of Germany and Japan. The inability of a regional ally to play such a function in the Middle East is not something to simply take at face value, however. Why, given the vast amounts of military and economic assistance along with close alliances, were states such as Iran (under the Shah), Israel, Saudi Arabia, Turkey, or Egypt (after Camp David) unable to play such a role?

Acharya has been one of the most effective advocates of a regional approach to global order which takes seriously the unique experience of non-Western areas of the world (Acharya 2007, 2014a). Acharya's influential (2014a) call for a global IR centered the experience of regions and the expertise of area studies, calling for "the acknowledgement of regional diversity and agency." Acharya conceptualizes regions "neither as wholly self-contained entities, nor as purely extensions of global dynamics," and articulates a compelling logic by which the study of regions within global politics centers the role of area studies at the heart of the discipline (Acharya 2014a: 650). These "regional worlds" are less predicated on hegemony than on local diversity and interaction, and typically have long historical roots rather than being artifacts of post–World War II American hegemony. It is not only the Middle East which is "porous" at its borders; all regions share this feature, as regions blur into one another in ways which push against the exclusionary logic of a world fragmenting into closed trade and political blocs (Acharya 2014a).

The tension between realist, neoliberal, and constructivist conceptions of region has significant implications not only for theory but also for the people and states who make up the ostensible regions. The experience of regionalism from within those regions rarely matches the theories or expectations from the top down (Bilgin 2004; Hazbun 2017). Regionalism in the Middle East has largely been about strengthening the existing states rather than delegating their functions for the purposes of integration (Hameiri 2013; Debre 2020; Heydemann and Lynch 2024). It has also functioned far more effectively in the societal realm than at the interstate level, usually in opposition to the policy preferences of the region's states, with subnational forms of regionalization having far more purchase on politics than the formal state bargaining and economic liberalization emphasized in the literature on the EU. The very different theoretical approaches to the nature of US primacy and the role of regions in its imperium, in turn, have offered a host of novel thinking about hierarchy in world politics and the place of the Middle East within global structure (Lake 2009b; Mattern and Zarakol 2016; McConnaughy, Musgrave, and Nexon 2018; Ikenberry and Nexon 2019; Lynch and Mabon 2025).

Is There Value to Theorizing Regions?

The idea of comparing regions makes good sense from the vantage point of international relations that moves beyond the Cold War and the parsimony of neorealism. But comparative regional systems required a level of analytical precision which was rarely on offer. The attempt to turn bureaucratic convenience and physical geography into analytical category has always been fraught. It is one thing to use "Africa" as a shorthand for all the countries on the African continent; it is quite another to assume that there is some essential quality of African-ness that unites them all into a coherent universe of cases for the purpose of theory-building or policy analysis (Basedau 2020). From the perspective of a Middle East scholar, Latin America seems like an easier case for analysis as a region; from the standpoint of a Latin Americanist, the logic of grouping all of South America, the Caribbean, and the rest of the Americas is far less obvious (Hoffmann 2015). It is difficult to do more than shake one's head and laugh softly when reading Samuel Huntington attempt to divide the world into "civilizations" which act like states (the "Confucian-Islamic alliance" lives in infamy). But a great deal of more serious social science implicitly does the same.

The organization of the American academy (at least) into area studies centers and programs presumes that there is value to studying the Middle East, Asia, or Africa as a coherent whole – and a phenomenal amount of good work has been done based on that premise. As early as 1960, Davison declared that nobody knows where the Middle East is, and that it made little sense as an analytical category, but that nonetheless an "agreement on arbitrary limits" would best facilitate scholarly progress. That compromise has largely continued ever since. It has held, in part, as an act of power: area studies, originating in colonialism and developing through the American academy, imposed order on the world in part through an act of definitional power. Area studies, in their original incarnation, meant American scholars studying foreign lands in the implicit or explicit pursuit of American national interests; American structural power can be seen in the internalization of those definitions by actors, scholars, and states within the regions it defined by fiat.

Why would scholarship based on faulty ontological assumptions have value? First, regions typically do have at least some common features which create *economies of scale* for the acquisition of expertise and knowledge. The legacies of the Ottoman Empire may not explain everything about the trajectory of the modern Middle East, but one can learn a lot about an entire broad swathe of the world by studying Ottoman institutions, practices, languages, and histories. The entire Middle East might not be Muslim, or speak Arabic, but mastering that religion and language will prove useful across several dozen countries in ways that it will not prove as useful in most others. This is the sentiment of Bayat (2013), who wearily concludes that even if the states of the Middle East don't have that much in common, they have more in common with each other than they do with states in other regions. I certainly feel more at home visiting a new Arab country than I do when working in Senegal or Uganda, even if the contexts are not identical.

Second, regions may prove useful analytical categories because *external powers use them to organize their foreign policies*. Global powers such as the United States have organized their foreign policy around such concepts, and through practice and power have created a uniformity which becomes naturalized over decades of repetition and normalization. When the United States and the Soviet Union treat the Middle East – or Africa, Asia, or Latin America – as coherent entities which require and reward a consistent foreign policy, then those policies can in turn shape the region in that direction. For example, once Washington has decided that the protection of oil and Israel requires the suppression of public opinion in one set of states assumed to be deeply hostile, then its support of autocratic regimes will create a self-reinforcing reality of a uniquely undemocratic region even if this was not grounded in history or culture. Entire bureaucracies and foreign policy communities have emerged which serve as vector points for policy engagement and practice; the Gulf might have less in common with the Levant than the term "Middle East" suggests, but in Washington it is at least covered by the same State Department desk officers and studied by the same think tanks.

Third, regions may *emerge endogenously* through political contestation and practice as regional powers – state or non-state – advance identity proposals to legitimate their ambitions and generate ideational power. As Section 4 details, Nasser's promotion of pan-Arabism in the 1950s, for example, intentionally constructed the Arab world as the appropriate and necessary site for "Arab" politics to happen. By constructing an identity narrative rooted in anti-colonialism, Palestine, and Arab unity, Nasser and his rivals combined to establish a distinctive playing field in which those issues mattered more within the region than outside of it – and, even more, having a stake in those (and only those) issues defined membership within the region. A state which opted for good relations with Israel in those years might have many qualities objectively associated with Arabness, but would be ostracized from Arab politics. Southeast Asia may have had no prior history as a region, but interaction through ASEAN and shared concerns with China may have generated a sense of region which had not previously existed (Thompson 2013).

Finally, regions may gain their value purely through the long-term structuring effects of the *confluence of money, power, and interest* (Cumings 1997). As Said (1978) observed, power constitutes not only knowledge about a subject but also the very object to be studied. Decisions by foundations, governments, and universities to organize knowledge in a particular way generate self-fulfilling dynamics which shape how graduate students are trained, where they publish, how they are hired, and what they teach. The Ford Foundation, SSRC, and the Department of Education may have made different decisions about how to divide the world in the late 1940s and early 1950s – adding South Asia and the East African coast to the Middle East, for instance, or placing North Africa within the rest of the African continent – and those regional borders might today feel natural and obvious, buttressed by generations of scholarly networks, expertise, and publication patterns. Succeeding within the field of Middle East studies might then today require familiarity with Swahili and Pashtu in addition to Arabic, Turkish, Hebrew, Kurdish, and Persian.

Still, as Eckstein (1975) long ago noted, for regions to make sense as analytical units, they must have sufficient common characteristics that differen-tiate them from other regions. Perhaps that is the case for some regions, perhaps not. But what about the Middle East? The Middle East today typically is understood to include the majority Arab states defined by membership in the Arab League (with a few, such as Mauritania and Djibouti, typically left out or at least ignored), Iran, Israel, and Turkey. This makes sense to many casual observers based on routine practice and regular usage in the media. It similarly makes sense to many political scientists accustomed to the division of know-ledge production into tidy regional packages which facilitate comparison or compartmentalization. But it does not quite make sense that it combines thinly populated oil-rich monarchies with massive industrialized northern African states, or that it includes a member of NATO alongside Qaddafi's eccentric Libya, or that it includes Israel's settler colonialist semi-democracy alongside Arab autocracies. Certain subregions make more sense based on the various criteria articulated in the literature: the Maghreb (North Africa), the Arabian Peninsula, the post-Ottoman countries of the Levant. But the Middle East?

It would be in a sense trivial to suggest that what unites the Middle East as a coherent world region is its place within global politics, from the colonial scramble of the European great powers to the bipolar structure of the Cold War to the post-1990 American crafting of a global imperium (Buzan and Waever 2003; Koch 2017). It clearly is that. But there's more. What puts actual coherence into this externally defined region is the emergence of a common set of stakes, actors, forms of power, and identities formulated through shared experience of intermittent transnationalized conflict. It may not be identical throughout, but its members have more in common than non-members. As Asaf Bayat puts it, "the Middle East, one may suggest, holds enough coherence to allow for addressing meaningful analytical questions, even though all this ultimately depends on what sort of analytical questions we wish to raise and what aspect of social life we have in mind" (Bayat 2013: 261). All of us in the business of Middle East political science proceed as if this were true. But is it?

At one level, the answer is yes – and the implications for academic training, language acquisition, and field research are clear. The best political science – and, more broadly, the best scholarship – is done by scholars who are deeply grounded in the country or area they study. Knowledge of the language, history, culture, and physical geography enables what has been called an "ethnographic sensibility," the ability to intuitively understand the significance and meaning of political events, discourse, and institutions. The efflorescence of Middle East political science of the last several decades has been rooted in the large-scale training and efforts of scholars who have combined rigorous methodologies drawn from general disciplines with that kind of local knowledge. But in a sense, this does not answer the question: why does local knowledge imply "region"? What actual local knowledge of, say, Yemen does a scholar have after spending a decade studying Amazigh politics in Morocco? Why would becoming an expert on Yemen necessarily require training in "Middle East" – and, indeed, what are the costs of such training (such as the exclusion of influences across the Indian Ocean and the East African coast)? Does a grounding in Middle East Studies strengthen one's understanding of Morocco more than deep study of French West Africa? Perhaps subregions are the answer, and relatively coherent smaller groupings of states which share a great deal of culture, history, and geography – the Levant, the Gulf, the Maghreb – do not need to be aggregated into a "Middle East." But this too is problematic: what, then, explains the shared engagement with the question of Palestine across subregions, or the patterns of protest diffusion (and non-diffusion) in the 2011 Arab uprisings?

The shared security complexes, historical legacies, shared language, and common political issues emphasized by international relations theory are not enough to capture the true distinctiveness of the Middle East. While each of those approaches illuminates an aspect of the region, all ultimately fall short of capturing the whole. But they point the way toward how to think about the Middle East as some form of region. Ideas, organizations, institutions, interests, and identities have all evolved over the course of a century in response to the distinctive forms of embeddedness of the Middle East into not only geopolitical conflict but also entrenched hierarchies. The particular nature of the Middle East's incorporation as a region into the global order – as a "subordinate international order," as Binder (1958) so evocatively labeled it – contributed to the isomorphism of its political institutions, economic arrangements, and social movements.

The Middle East does not actually make intuitive sense as a coherent region, then, but then no region really does. All regions are political constructs, designed for particular reasons and reflecting particular constellations of identity, power, and interest (Bilgin 2004). Scholars of virtually every world region have criticized the artificiality of categorization of their region. Southeast Asianists point out that their "region" is incredibly diverse across almost every dimension (Pepinsky 2023); Latin Americanists point out that Brazil is not Spanish-speaking; among Africanists, it is even something of a running joke to insist that Africa is not a country. But one must start somewhere.

But where? When Admiral Mahan famously coined the term "Middle East," he did not bother to specify its boundaries; most early usages of the term incorporated India and viewed it as part of the British colonial patrimony (Khalil 2016; Crouzet 2022). For the eminent historian Nikki Keddie (1973), the Middle East referred to "the area stretching from Morocco to Afghanistan, and is roughly equivalent to the area of the first wave of Muslim conquests plus Anatolia." For the US State Department, for decades it included the Gulf and the Levant, but not North Africa. The inaugural issue of *The Middle East Journal* in 1947 featured a map of the region extending to India and most of central Asia (Kurzman 2007). In 1981, William Thompson observed that of six major studies of the Middle Eastern regional system, none included the same set of states. In 1992, Bernard Lewis speculated (but got few takers) that with the collapse of the Soviet Union, the Middle East had "resumed its historical dimensions" by reclaiming the six newly independent central Asian republics: "Samarkand and Bukhara are, after all, as much a part of the historic Middle East as Esfahan and Damascus." Louise Fawcett's influential edited volume on the International Relations of the Middle East extends the standard definition of the region to include Somalia and Mauritania.

For all of that confusion, people seem to think they know where the Middle East is – and universities are certainly organized as if they do. This has more to do with funding and institutional practice than with intellectual merits. The standard definition of the Middle East was consolidated with the US Department of Education's Title VI Area Studies grants and includes the Arab states (usually defined as the Arab League membership), Israel, Iran, and Turkey. This collection of states represents geographical contiguity, of a sort, but without clear justifications for where its members begin and end. It lacks coherence historically, linguistically, ethnically, and religiously. The members of the Arab League may be "Arab states," but that is itself a political construct (see Section 3) which erases wide variations in ethnic identity, such as the Amazigh populations across the Maghreb and the Kurdish populations spread across the Levant. Turkey and Iran are of obvious political and strategic importance to the other states included in the Middle East, but each is also a central player in at least one other region (Turkey into the Balkans and the Caucasus (and increasingly Africa), Iran into the Persianate world of Central Asia and Afghanistan).

The linguistic diversity is not simply the non-Arabic languages (Kurdish, Hebrew, Farsi, Turkish, Amazigh) but extends even to the Arabic-speaking countries. I will long recall my dismay on first visiting Morocco to realize that my Levantine Arabic was useless and that I would be better off using my atrocious French, and my delight at the recently initiated presence of Tamazight as a third language on most road signs. In Tunisia, I found that Islamists were far more likely to be able to communicate with me in Modern Standard Arabic than any other segment of society, including many in the secular, educated elite who preferred French or English, while I found taxi drivers from the south of the country incomprehensible. On my first visit to Qatar, my cab driver stared at me baffled when I asked to go to my hotel in Arabic; a lovely young man from Sri Lanka, he had little difficulty driving a taxi in Doha with facility in only English.

It is telling that the US military uses a different definition of the Middle East than does the State Department or most universities. For military operations, getting things right is a matter of life or death – whether or not those decisions are academically defensible or historically valid. The Central Command extends to Afghanistan, Djibouti, Eritrea, Ethiopia, Kenya, Pakistan, Somalia, and Sudan – while excluding (until quite recently) North Africa and Israel. That makes good sense when one considers the role of US military bases on the Arabian Peninsula for running the air wars and logistics for Afghanistan, or the deep and escalating integration of Gulf states in the political and military affairs of Eastern Africa. On the flip side, when the United States sought to took the lead in combat operations in Libya in 2011, its primary military organization for the Middle East played no role.

Each of these groupings of states represented a confluence of geopolitical and local factors of quite recent vintage. Prior to the twentieth century, the Ottoman Empire expanded across not only much of what is now "the Middle East" but also deep into the Balkans and central Europe, but by the time that the regions crystallized institutionally those Christian provinces had been hived off for decades. By the 1800s, most of the Arabian Peninsula coast was functionally part of British India, while the three states of the Maghreb were fully integrated into the French Empire (Algeria actually becoming legally part of France). The connections between Arabia and East Africa ran deep and seemed completely natural based on geography and trade connections; Oman ruled Zanzibar for centuries, and to this day Swahili is a common language across many of the Arab Gulf states (Mathews 2024). Arabs from the Maghreb and the Mashreq viewed each other with suspicion and distance, and could not even communicate with each other in colloquial Arabic. The grouping we now call the Middle East mostly followed the logic of great power politics and the Cold War rather than historical precedent or material economic or political connectivity.

The "Near East" represented the imperial concerns of the United Kingdom, where the Arabian Peninsula, Egypt, and the Red Sea represented the key connector between India and Europe and a potential source of threat from France and other rival powers (Low 2020; Crouzet 2022), while the Ottoman Caliphate represented a potential rival for the loyalties of Indian Muslims. The United States had less parochial concerns as it turned its attention to the region after World War II. For Washington, the entire region was a distinct part of a global battleground in the struggle against the Soviet Union – with non-Arab Iran a critical part of the security architecture protecting the flow of oil from the Gulf, and Israel a politically unavoidable part of the security and political challenges across the Levant and the Gulf. The allure of pan-Arabism in the 1950s and 1960s forced America's hand in accepting a broad regional definition, because the issues of the day – especially Palestine but also the wars of national liberation such as in Algeria – objectively were self-evidently interconnected and needed to be dealt with through a regional lens.

That definition was locked in place institutionally by the US government through the 1958 National Defense Education Act, with the Title VI program designed to support area studies centers and foreign language training. Top American research institutions imported star scholars from European institutions to lead these new centers and institutes, bringing along many European colonial assumptions about the region (Lockman 2003, 2016). The emphasis on language training and field research encouraged the scholars trained in these centers toward an ethnographic sensibility, initially, even as foundation funders and US government consumers tried to push them toward the social and behavioral sciences (Khalil 2016; Lockman 2016). It is, as Rafael (1994) points out, a fascinating contradiction that Middle East Studies (like all the area studies) was founded based on Orientalist conceptions of regional essentialism while cultivating generations of scholars committed to combatting Orientalism, and that generations of scholars trained to oppose US imperialism depended on US government funding and university systems shaped by those official incentives.

For the first several decades, the connection to national security and US interests was clear, with a heavy emphasis on language training, history, and religion producing generations of talented scholars with a particular skill set (Cumings 1997; Mitchell 2003; Khalil 2016). As a result, scholars of the Middle East developed deep expertise about the cultures, languages, history, and politics of the countries in that tightly defined area. But the definition of regions had costs: they were not expected to know much of anything about sub-Saharan Africa or Afghanistan and Pakistan, no matter how important those places might be to the issues they were studying – or, down the road, they would become to American policy interests. The impact of such divides would be laid bare by the transnational networks of al-Qaeda in the 1990s and 2000s, which emerged out of the Middle East but carried out its earliest attacks in Africa and took harbor in Sudan and Afghanistan – all virtually invisible to those who studied the Middle East.

In the 1970s, Middle East Studies was broadly transformed by the political firestorms surrounding the 1967 war and the rise of pro-Palestinian and anti-Vietnam activism in the academy (Hajjar and Niva 1997; Lockman 2003). This new politicization problematized the previously quite tight connections between academic and the intelligence agencies, as scholars of the Middle East followed suit with those working in Asia, Africa, and Latin America in rejecting funding and consultation from US government sources (some of them at least; most continued to pursue Title VI and FLAS awards even if they steered clear of the CIA). As many Middle East scholars celebrated – and right-wing critics bemoaned – younger scholars of Arab origin increasingly joined the ranks of Middle East Studies. They brought with them a more critical politics, far more skeptical of connections to American foreign policy and far more critical of Israel. They also brought deep, intimate knowledge of their own societies and languages which challenged the expertise claimed by earlier generations of scholars. In terms of the definition of the Middle East, this had dual, often conflicting, implications. On the one hand, many scholars of Arab origin worked from a presumption of the natural identity of the region as Arab – strengthening the core definition of the region while politicizing and often rejecting the legitimate presence of Israel, Turkey, and Iran (as well as of minorities such as Kurds or Amazigh). On the other hand, many of the leftist scholars among these ranks identified more broadly with the global South and anticolonial struggles, leading them to challenge artificial barriers between regional political struggles against common colonial enemies.

This articulation of the Middle East within the academy was "naturalized" broadly through the circulation of maps, educational practices, bureaucratic routine, and popular discourse (Culcasi 2010). Few could argue with Said's (1979, 1981) brilliant demonstration of how "the Middle East" became in the popular imagination a shorthand for violence, corrupt oil barons, and religious fanaticism, with an assumed commonality binding together all the "Orient" from Morocco and Yemen to India (and beyond, where convenient). The distinctions blurred in these popular visions such that it made intuitive sense that historical events in, say, Afghanistan might be taken as a reliable guide to current events in Lebanon. Such crude generalizations rarely gained traction in the academy, but their shadows could be recognized in the assumptions underlying even quite sophisticated research. Take, for example, Steven Fish's *Are Muslims Different* which aggregates public opinion surveys and other quantitative data from across multiple "Middle Eastern" (and not other) countries to draw inferences about Islam, a global religion with a billion adherents spread far beyond the Middle East (see Section 4). And they would recur in the early days after 9/11, when a legion of analysts emerged to attribute jihadism to "Muslim rage" or to the pathologies of a decontextualized Arab world.

It is telling that the questioning of the definition of "regions" and "areas" primarily has taken place in moments of profound global structural change – the end of the Cold War and rise of globalization (1990s) and, perhaps, today's decline of US primacy. Middle East Studies had to adapt to the end of the Cold War and the post-1990 emergence of a discourse of American primacy (Hajjar and Niva 1997). The SSRC and ACLS ended their decades-long support for area studies centers as globalization took center stage, while the Ford Foundation, the SSRC, and the Mellon Foundation spearheaded initiatives to "rethink area studies" (Bilgin 2004; Kurzman 2007). The idea that globalization had reduced the importance of areas and had made "areas more porous, less bounded, less fixed" (Cumings 1997) became a central pillar of the reorganiza-tion of funding priorities and programming. The SSRC, for instance, deter-mined in the mid-1990s "that a number of discrete and separated 'area committees,' each focused on a single world region, is not the optimum structure for providing new insights and theories suitable for a world in which the geographic units of analysis are neither static nor straightforward" (Prewitt 1993). In 2016, the SSRC published another important collection entitled *Middle East Studies for the New Millennium*, the product of over fifteen years of collective work funded by multiple foundations, which once again sought to find purchase for area expertise in an age of declining US primacy and shifting academic priorities (Shami and Miller-Idriss 2016).

The Middle East continued to receive attention, whatever was happening with other areas and regions. This was not necessarily a good thing, of course; public discourse was often dominated by journalists, pundits, and a mixed bag of think-tankers, while even the academic realm became a stomping ground for terrorism experts, war grifters, and neo-Orientalists. Still, the frequent wars and crises in the region ensured that the Middle East remained a primary focus of US government interest and funding, given the insatiable demand for a modicum of language skills and basic cultural knowledge needed to staff the occupation of Iraq and the far-flung networks of the global war on terror. Critics of Middle East Studies might complain that area experts were too critical of US foreign policy or too hostile toward Israel, but few could argue that the US government did not need well-trained experts conversant in regional languages and politics. The debate over whether Middle East scholars should actively serve US inter-ests has been a consistent through-thread for decades, in some ways peaking during the occupation of Iraq when some anthropologists served American counterinsurgency forces in the Human Terrain System – what Roberto Gonzalez termed "mercenary anthropology" – a common issue in other areas too, of course, especially in Asian Studies during the Vietnam years (Cumings 1997).

It is worth acknowledging local agency in these definitional battles, as Section 4 does at length. But such local agency can be observed even at the geopolitical level. The interests and identities of local powers in defining the region are perhaps best seen in the exclusion of Africa. The project of pan-Arabism pointedly differentiated itself from pan-Africanism, splitting potential solidarities across the Global South. For all the colonial roots of this exclusion (see Section 2), we must recognize the deep anti-Black racism and legacies of slavery across much of the Arab world which fueled these divisions. Arabizing post-colonial elites in North Africa advanced national projects against both former European colonial powers and against the Black African countries to their south – erasing Amazigh populations along the way. Southern European elites, keen to join Europe and to differentiate themselves from their North African counterparts across the Mediterranean, pushed hard to create legal and institutional barriers – a project which had particular salience around the place of Algeria, which until 1962 was legally part of France and had a solid claim on that basis to membership in the European Community (Brown 2022).

But is there more to the grouping of states in the Middle East than just geopolitical convenience? Are there common features across these states which could plausibly justify their inclusion as well as the exclusion of other possible members? Asef Bayat (2013) concludes his reflections on the variety of experience across a diverse region with the pragmatic note that in the end, the countries of the Middle East have more in common with each other than with non-Middle Eastern states. Do they? Do the states of the Maghreb (which clearly do share common cultural, institutional, linguistic, ethnic, and political characteristics with each other) have more in common with the states of the Levant or Gulf than they do with those of Francophone West Africa? Are the Gulf states (which really do share a great many common political, cultural, economic, and institutional characteristics) today really more comparable to Egypt than to Singapore or other entrepots of global finance and commerce? What does Turkey, an advanced industrial democracy (of sorts) and NATO member, have in common with the collapsed states of the Arab interior? What are the effects of the rise of English as the primary language of the globalized elites of the Gulf – or the choice by several of those countries to normalize with Israel in the absence of a resolution to the Palestinian issue – mean for their membership in the Middle East?

Hinnebusch (2015), in his magisterial study of the international relations of the Middle East, lays out several key differences which might impact the region relative to other parts of the world: Ottoman legacies, the distinctive nature of colonial penetration and uneven state development, the mismatch between nation and state, the unusually high level of external interest. The Middle East, he argues, has been shaped by the Israeli–Palestinian conflict in ways that non-Middle Eastern states have not been, has very distinctive patterns of sectarian Sunni–Shi'a polarization, and is shaped by the distinctive concerns of pan-Arabism. This approach mirrors recent trends in IR theories of hierarchy, which similarly place significant causal weight on the distinctive ways the Middle East was incorporated into the global order (Lake 2009a). The analysis of regional similarity based on the historical sociology of dependent state formation arguably makes more sense within the Levantine core than it does for the Gulf or North Africa, however, to say nothing of Turkey, Iran, and Israel;

all had very different experiences of colonialism and entered the global order at different times and by different mechanisms.

Particularly interesting in this regard is the conceptualization offered by Nile Green (2014) of at least three civilizationally distinct regions within the area often called the Middle East: a Mediterranean region connecting the Levant with the North African coast and western Turkey; a Persianate region encompassing Iran and much of central Asia and parts of South Asia; and an Indian Ocean region connecting the Arabian Peninsula with East Africa and the Indian subcontinent. Green notes the intellectual costs of these categorizations: "The study of Iran, Afghanistan, the Gulf, and the Arabian Peninsula have been the most obvious victims of this conceptual restriction through the elision of their formative and ongoing connections to the continental and maritime "farther east" of Central Asia and the Indian Ocean." This conception beautifully captures the historical, civilizational connections which might plausibly make a region – but, at the same time, has virtually no resonance with how contemporary politics and identities are organized.

The trend across the literature on subregions in recent years is telling. The rapidly growing field of Gulf studies has increasingly explored and excavated the Arabian peninsula's historical and ongoing connections to India and South Asia, from the era of British Empire through today's patterns of labor migration (Khanna, Renard, and Vora 2020). Turkish studies have explored the shifting domestic conceptions of Turkey's regional identity, with neo-Ottomanists recalling the long history of the empire and cosmopolitans looking to become part of Europe (Hintz 2019). Maghreb Studies have increasingly looked to the problematic nature of the Sahara as a dividing line, particularly with the rise of Amazigh studies highlighting the ongoing life across the supposed division (Hannoum 2022). This section builds on these subregional trends as well as broader trends within the IR literature on regions and regionalism to situate the Middle East more effectively.

Orientalism, Political Science, and the Middle East

Here, it is worth returning briefly to the question of Orientalism and its relationship to the area studies. Largely due to the influence of Said, Middle East Studies, more than other world regions, has emphasized Orientalism and the constitutive effects of centuries of the colonial production of knowledge. Each region's area studies have confronted the artificiality of regions in different ways, slaying different dragons and fighting different prejudices. In the Middle East, the specter of Orientalism – both the academic tradition and Edward Said's influential critique – has been particularly central. The Middle

East is often presented as a uniquely conflict-prone region of the world. In the popular imagination, a whole range of pathologies are uniquely associated with the region: autocracy, violence, fanaticism, gender oppression, and more. Such long-standing tropes have been the subject of a vast array of criticism, inspired by the work of Said on the discursive work of an essentializing Orientalism.

As valuable as that body of work remains, especially in laying bare the relations between colonialism and scholarship, there are reasons to question such a perspective when it comes to the definition of regions. Put bluntly, the Middle East as a discrete region is barely a century old – and there is little agreement about which countries it encompasses, or why. How can we assume timeless, unique pathologies when we cannot even agree on which countries or peoples it describes? And why would those essentializing discourses apply uniquely to the Middle East, as opposed to other colonized area such as India and Africa? Attributing this to "Orientalism," despite the undoubted racism of the colonial gaze, is unsatisfying. Similarly racist Othering is prevalent across other world regions, and does not clearly differentiate the Middle East from Africa, India, or Asia. Nor do common, seemingly intuitive markers actually denote what they seem: the Middle East is not identical with Arabic-speaking, it does not end or begin at the boundaries of the former Ottoman Empire, it is not exclusively or uniquely Islamic, and its geographical proximity is largely a function of where one begins and stops looking at the map. A wide range of other regional configurations could have been produced by racist versions of Orientalism; what concerns us is this one.

I would argue that political science diverged rather dramatically from other disciplines during the subsequent decades. Most of the disciplines within Middle East Studies were profoundly affected by Edward Said's critique of Orientalism and their scholarship took an increasingly politicized, often identitarian turn. Political science had far less interest in Said's critiques, though. Instead, as I demonstrate in Section 5, political scientists of the Middle East became consumed with the "area studies controversy" and the challenge posed by advocates of a universal social theory to specialists in particular regions and countries. Modernization theory may have begun with Orientalist assumptions, but it assumed the potential to reach a modern Westernized ideal. Where other disciplines saw their best and brightest young scholars delve deeply into Said and critical theory to investigate positionality, historical memory, discourse, and identity, the rising generation of political science turned to the discipline's preferred methods – often quantitative or formal, with even the qualitative work almost always rigidly positivist. There is some irony that the most influential attack on Middle East Studies in this era, Martin Kramer's (2001) *Ivory Towers in the Sand*, almost exclusively used examples from political science in his bill of complaints against Edward Said's alleged perversion of Middle East Studies; those who Kramer most directly critiqued were actually by far the least influenced by his bête noire.

Political science has been perhaps the discipline least impacted by Said and the critique of Orientalism. But, as detailed in Section 5, it has its own set of problems driven by assumptions about the region. To briefly preview here, the literature on the Middle East has for decades been relatively parochial and insular, with a deep study of the region or its individual countries generating vast expertise but often not informing broader disciplinary theories. Many studies of Middle East politics assume a universe of only Middle Eastern cases, with little justification for establishing those boundaries. Why, though, should a study of democracy and autocracy limit its inquiry to the two dozen member states of the Arab League when the challenges of democratization are fully global? Why should the effects of oil rents be studied within the Arab world, without attention to comparable oil producers in Africa, Central Asia, Latin America, or North America? How could we measure the difference of the Middle East from other regions in terms of conflict prevalence if we don't know which countries belong in the Middle East (Sørli, Gleditsch, and Strand 2005)? I would argue that rather than simply broadening the aperture of our datasets to be more cross-regionally comparative (as important as that would be), we need to think carefully about why it seems to make intuitive sense to group together the various subregions into a single region.

3 The Middle East from the Outside In

The Middle East, like other world regions, emerged in its current form in response to the spread of colonialism and then its transition into the Cold War. It is, of course, not unique in this. Southeast Asian Studies has faced remarkably similar questions and doubts over its history (Acharya 2014b). The definition of the "Asia" region after World War II evolved in line with US strategic thinking, with an "East Asia" threatened with overrun by Communist China giving way after 1975 to a "Pacific Rim" which allowed Washington to put Vietnam behind it (Cumings 1997: 8). The level of interest Washington had in the region because of the Vietnam War had a negative effect on the quality of scholarship which would ring familiar to students of the Middle East. This section explores the outside-in dimensions of the construction of the Middle East as a region, focusing on the configuration of global interests and power relations which resolved around this particular grouping of states being treated as an analytical and political unit. The following section reverses the lens to examine the inside-out dynamics of regional actors, state and non-state, contesting the definition of the region and advancing identity proposals in line with their interests.

The "Middle East" as a regional concept is barely a half-century old, and virtually impossible to even imagine without the context of global war, local violent political struggle, and transregional connectivity. During earlier historical eras, European powers might have viewed the "Orient" as an undifferentiated, unchanging Muslim world, or viewed the Ottoman Empire as a worthy or unworthy competitor in the great game of colonial competition. But while Orientalist imaginaries undoubtedly colored imperial approaches to what would become the Middle East, there was nothing unchanging about the newly conceived region. External powers developed highly differentiated and subtle understandings of particularities of regions and subregions. Visions of the Middle East as a discrete unit took centuries to develop out of the particular discourses and interests associated with the British and French imperial projects, the racist differentiation of the Arab regions from "Black" Africa, and the concerns about the potential for the Ottoman Caliphate to mobilize the world's Muslims outside the nation-state project. Even more to the point, the "Middle East" emerged from the carnage of World War I and World War II, and came of age in the early Cold War at a time when Washington's political arena became truly global and the confluence of oil, Israel, and strategic location put the region inexorably at the center of the national security agenda.

The Middle East which emerged from this external structuring was not created out of nothing, of course. Most of what became this region had for centuries past been unified under Ottoman rule and shared what Hodgson called an Islamicate civilization. As Wyrtzen brilliantly demonstrates, the region which emerged from the aftermath of World War I and the internal convulsions of the late Ottoman Empire was a deeply interconnected one (Wyrtzen 2022). Lands as distant as Morocco's Rif and the Levantine cities of Beirut and Damascus struggled against the same French colonial power, mutually inspired by one another's successes and battling against an opponent wielding the same technologies and discourses as those developed in its of Algeria. While the trope that the colonial powers simply invented the states of the Middle East from whole cloth is wildly exaggerated and deeply misleading, it is more true to say that the borders and domestic institutions established in the colonial period reflected the exigencies of European great power competition and the remaining legacies of Ottoman rule.

The Middle East might have developed in a truly regional direction after World War I, had the British delivered on their promise to the Hashemites to create a unified Arab Kingdom in the former lands of the Ottoman Empire. Perhaps that Kingdom, with the oil fields of Iraq and the holy places of Mecca and Medina (which were still held by the Kingdom of the Hijaz, not yet conquered by the Saudis), would have become the core of a regional bloc able to compete with the other world powers on their own terms. But that was not to be. The Middle East has never been allowed to develop such core states or regional orders in the absence of international intervention. Where other regions saw the emergence of great powers through conquest and competition, in the Middle East the imperial powers routinely blocked the consolidation or expansion of power by regional actors (Lustick 1997; Hinnebusch 2015). Of all the region's states, only Saudi Arabia emerged through the standard Tilly-approved process of expansion and conquest – and its expansion was, in turn, blocked primarily by British military protection of its local allies along the Gulf coast and, later, in Transjordan and Iraq.

The history of the late Ottoman Empire helped to shape the potential cultural unity of the emergent Middle East region. The Islamic identity of the Ottoman Empire was in large part a function of the loss of its European provinces and its emergent competition with British India. The Arab identity of the Levant similarly emerged in opposition to the centralizing and Turkifying efforts of a reforming empire, with the so-called "Great Arab Revolt" unfolding as an integral part of British wartime strategy rather than any sort of indigenous uprising. The Gulf was shaped in large part by British interests in maintaining shipping routes from colonial India and competing with the Ottomans over the loyalty of Muslims within their empire. Aden and the Red Sea linking the Hajj and the Suez Canal shipping route loomed larger than the emirates along the Gulf in the earlier period (Low 2022). The discovery of the value of oil, of course, then added a deeper layer onto the military and strategic value of the region, incorporating Iran and Iraq as producers with the Gulf and Red Sea as key transit points. War and the prospect of violence always loomed over the British calculation of their interests and their construction of the "Near East" as a critical object of strategic control.

The Maghreb's place within the broader French imperial system similarly challenges the uniqueness of any particular "Middle Eastern" experience with its colonialism (Neep 2012). The brutal pacification and incorporation of Algeria over more than a century culminated in the bloody 1954–1962 war of independence, a war of national liberation which profoundly shaped every aspect of Algerian politics and society. But similar imperial violence marked French colonialism in Asia, most notably Vietnam, with similarly bloody and globally significant impacts. Colonial officials from Algeria and Morocco played a key role in constructing French rule in Syria and Lebanon (Neep 2012; Hibri 2021). France dragooned soldiers for the world wars from Africa to the Caribbean to the Middle East, though with clear racial gradations in terms of their treatment.

The common denominator in these patterns of state formation is that there was not a single template of colonial rule, a single pattern of economic incorporation, or even a common experience of mismatch between state and nation. The experiences of the Maghreb with French colonialism looked nothing like British control of the Arabian Peninsula's coast, and neither resembled the post–World War I creation of the new states of the Levant. What structured them all was a shared emplacement within a global security order which identified key threats emanating from the Middle East which largely resonated with indigenous political developments: anti-colonialism, hostility to Israel, and the demand for Arab unity.

The Great Game, the "Near East," and the Maghreb

The origin story of the "Middle East" region – then named the "Near East" – begins with London's need to connect its imperial possessions in India back to the home island (Adelson 1995; Foliard 2020). British imperial interests were not limited to the current definition of the Middle East. Instead, they involved complex connections among India, the Hajj regions of Mecca and Medina, the oil entrepots of Iran and the ports of the Arabian peninsula, and Egypt's Suez Canal. In the run-up to World War I, one of Britain's greatest strategic fears was that the Ottoman Caliph would successfully mobilize the Muslims of the Raj to a jihad against the Allied Powers – a fear which assumed the unity of a broad Muslim region which transcended the Arab world or even the physical reach of the Ottoman Empire.

As Willis (2009) notes, the British Empire did not divide its imperial territories into neat regions such as Near East and South Asia, as we do today. Much of the Gulf fell under the jurisdiction of the India Colonial Office: "the definition of imperial India was not restricted to the Indian 'subcontinent' but was defined in relation to imperial sovereignty. Britain incorporated hundreds of semi-independent polities along the Arabian peninsula into the Raj, and understood Aden as the westernmost point of India, governed by Bombay until finally being transferred to the British Colonial Office in 1937. The military forces of the Aden-based Middle East Command Britain established in the early 1960s were stationed in Kenya until its independence in 1963. Egypt was similarly governed out of the India Office; Lord Cromer, so central to the creation of modern Egypt, learned his profession in India as did so many other British colonial officials who shaped what would become the Middle East.

The French, for their part, sought to demarcate and divide the Maghreb from the eastern, British-, and Italian-owned North African coast and from Black West Africa. As Hannoum (2022) documents, French colonial anthropologists generated phenomenal amounts of supposedly scientific knowledge designed to prove the essential difference between the Sahara Desert in the west from its extensions in the south of Libya. Racial differentiation, as elsewhere in the empire, played a central role in determining which areas became the Maghreb and which became French West Africa. Those colonial impositions would have long-lasting effects on race relations and conceptions of citizenship in the post-independence Maghreb countries.

The British and the French largely succeeded in blocking other European powers from gaining access to the areas which made up their colonial domains. Germany and other competitors looked further south into sub-Saharan Africa, or into Asia, leaving the Levant, Gulf, and North Africa largely uncontested within the Great Game (the less said about Italy's disastrous, near-genocidal incursion into Libya and the Horn of Africa, the better). This was less true in Iran, however, where Russia repeatedly sought to expand its influence, or in Afghanistan, which at the time was far less obviously excluded from the regional domain.

World Wars and the Formation of the Modern Middle East

World War I is often taken as the origin story for the modern Middle East, and for good reason – if one is only looking at the Levant and Egypt. That war should be understood not only as a European war but as an Imperial war in which the great powers generated manpower and resources from their colonial possessions. One of the unintended effects of this mobilization was that soldiers from far-flung colonial possessions came into direct contact for the first time, generating new potential for solidarities across the colonies. Anderson's (2021) account of the Egyptian Labor Corps documents one moment of such contact, as Egyptians found themselves fighting alongside Indians and Africans while discovering where the British actually ranked them within the racial hierarchies of the day. The French war effort brought together fighters from as far afield as Senegal and Martinique, shaping the political consciousness of such future luminaries as Leopold Senghor and Frantz Fanon. Such solidarities could have established the basis for a global anti-colonial identity not attached to region or nation. Instead, the push for national self-determination and the Mandate system rooted in racial hierarchies interrupted such emergent solidarities in favor of a system of nascent nation-states and regions more manageable by declining empires.

The Mandate period was crucial for defining the Middle East against other regions, even if that term was not yet in wide circulation (Wyrtzen 2022). Middle Eastern political figures, from the politicians of Egypt's Wafd to the Hashemite Faisal bin Hussein, prowled the halls of the Versailles conference and sought to shape the future of what they understood as a region. The League of Nations followed an implicitly racial logic in its classification of types of mandates, sorting them by region and placing the Levantine mandates of the former Ottoman Empire in a "semi-civilized" class which differentiated them from the uncivilized (i.e. Black) mandates of Africa. The French and British Middle Eastern mandates were ostensibly intended to provide tutelage toward the creation of modern states and democratic systems which would ultimately qualify them for independent statehood. Nationalists in these Arab mandates rarely challenged their elevation over the African "barbarians," even if they chafed at European domination and tutelage. In practice, both mandatory powers governed their new territories as colonies, imposing their preferred political and economic systems while facing down sometimes intense nationalist opposition with extreme violence.

The typical template for understanding the emergence of the modern Middle East heavily weights the experience of the Levant, in which France and Britain carved up the Arab provinces of the Ottoman Empire through a series of secret agreements (most famously, but not actually most importantly, Sykes-Picot). The regional shared identity of the Levant is difficult to dispute, given that these new states had quite recently been part of the same political order where borders did not exist and elites easily circulated. The Palestine mandate rapidly evolved into a distinctive conflict zone with the influx of Zionist immigration and the sequential battles to shape British colonial policy; no extra work needed to be done to make Palestinians part of that regional construct, since they had been so for many centuries. But it is important to recall that none of the other subregions of the Middle East followed this template: the Gulf was shaped through bargains between imperial Britain and local rulers seeking the upper hand over their rivals along the coast, and Saudi expansion in the interior; the Maghreb was shaped by long decades of French settler colonialism and transformational governance.

The connections between the Levant and the other major subregions of the Middle East in this period require a bit more careful attention. The inclusion of the Maghreb in the Middle East arguably resulted from the circulation of French colonial elites and practices from Algeria to Syria and Lebanon. The post– World War II departure of large Jewish communities from the Maghreb (as well as Iraq and Egypt) to Israel, and the systematic marginalization of the Amazigh communities by post-independence regimes shifted the subregion toward an

Arabophone identity which further facilitated connections to the Levant. So did the interest shown by major Arab powers such as Egypt in Algeria's war of national independence, which generated enduring connections between post-independence FLN elites and the Arab world. These connections were never fully solidified, however, as the Maghreb continued to be embedded within the Francophone community and economically oriented toward Europe through both trade and labor migration.

World War II upended some of these assumptions, but imperial practice remained deeply rooted in the previous era. The British ran much of the war out of Cairo, rather than out of India, which had transformative effects on Egypt while also cementing its strategic ties with the other subregions – the Maghreb, the Levant, and the Gulf (Jakes 2020). The American role in the North African campaigns increased demand for regional expertise in ways that would matter for the evolution of Middle East studies (Khalil 2016; Lockman 2016). The shift from coal to oil in the imperial British and US naval fleets dramatically escalated the global strategic importance of Saudi Arabia, Iran, and the Gulf, centering those oil producers in the war against Germany and Japan and then in the emergent global Cold War. Palestine, as ever, served as a unifying issue for the crystallization of a region, as concerns that rising Zionist immigration to Palestine could make Arabs and Muslims receptive to Nazi anti-Semitic appeals mirrored at a greater strategic scale the worry in the previous great war about an Ottoman Caliph promoting disloyalty among imperial Muslim subjects. Britain's final departure from India foreshadowed its near-simultaneous abandonment of the Palestine mandate. The French collapse pushed "France" out of Europe and into its empire, a stunning reversal. And the great battles between the Allies and the Nazis across North Africa forced a recognition of the strategic importance of the southern shores of the Mediterranean.

The Cold War, Pan-Arabism, and America's Middle East

Britain's hegemony over the definition of the Near East did not survive its late 1940s departure from India and Palestine; by the time it finally wrapped up its Gulf positions in 1971, the UK had long since ceased to be the dominant player in any part of the region. France too lost its core Middle Eastern positions with the 1956 Suez war fiasco and the bloody eight-year war of Algerian national liberation; while it attempted to sustain a Francophone Africa in the ensuing decades, it faded as a regional superpower. The "Middle East" became a primarily American conception, rooted in geopolitical competition with the Soviet Union and built upon different assumptions about what ultimately mattered (that the State Department retains a Bureau of Near East Affairs, despite this, remains a source of some bureaucratic amusement).

The rise of pan-Arabism in the 1950s (discussed in the next section) brought about perhaps the most clearly regionalized politics of any world region. The 1956 Suez Crisis showed the connections across subregions powerfully in the emerging "Middle East" region, as France supported the British–Israeli plans to seize the Suez Canal and undermine Nasser's new regime in large part because they saw pan-Arabism as supporting the Algerian war of national independence. The United States, for its part, forced Britain and France to withdraw from their positions in the Sinai in part for fear that being seen as siding with Israel would have catastrophic effects on America's position with the Arab world. In both cases, direct and indirect connections among the countries of the Middle East – but not beyond, and with Iran and Algeria necessarily included – played a critical role at the highest strategic level.

It is worth considering here the global effects of the Arab cold war, which were quite different in many ways from their effects on intra-regional dynamics. Western powers saw the potential alignment of pan-Arab regimes with the Soviet Union as a profound threat in the context of the broader Cold War, even if (or perhaps because) their real focus was anti-imperialism rather than any genuine support for Communism. But there was another, secondary effect of pan-Arabism that rebounded to the benefit of the Western powers. The focus on Arab unity came at the direct expense of broader global anti-colonial solidarity, blunting its revolutionary impact on the global stage. Nasser began as a core participant in Bandung and other foundational moments of the Non-Aligned Movement, while Maghreb states such as Algeria figured prominently in the global anti-colonial movement (Malley 1996; Byrne 2019). But Nasser grew jealous of African leaders such as Nkrumah and Senghor, and sought to define pan-Arabism in part against pan-Africanism, with racial animus and local political concerns driving Egypt and other pan-Arab regimes toward the more insular pan-Arab discourse.

The defeat of pan-Arabism after 1967 is typically seen as the consolidation of the state system and the emergence of a more normal, Realist form of regional international relations. This is both true and misleading. It is certainly the case that the creation of massive national security states fueled by the oil boom and dedicated to ensuring the survival of existing regimes dampened the ability of popular opinion to be heard on issues such as Palestine. But it is equally the case that Arab labor migration to the Gulf continued in this period, providing continuity in the underlying material foundations of regionalism while also serving as a transmission belt (both financial and ideational) for the rapid rise of Islamism across most of the region (Lacroix 2014; Medani 2022). The Iranian

Revolution and the Iran–Iraq war which followed, as well as the parallel civil war in Lebanon and rise of Hezbollah, further consolidated the Gulf's regional security complex in ways that connected it to the Levant.

Why did the United States care whether the Middle East was a region? In part because for the sake of its bureaucratic organization, but also because it pursued a stable set of interests in the Middle East over the course of nearly half a century which it viewed as core to its global security. It placed a particularly high value on the production and transportation of oil from the Gulf at sustainable prices, which was a core pillar of the Western capitalist system and the foundation of American hegemony within the West. It was committed to the survival and prosperity of Israel, primarily for domestic political reasons but also for strategic reasons in the post-1967 period. And, throughout, it was determined to prevent Soviet gains within the region, which it viewed as a proxy for the global balance of power in ways similar to the domino theory which kept it locked in Vietnam for so many bloody years. All of those core interests required that Washington work to sustain the status quo of friendly regimes who would ensure both the flow of oil and Israel's security despite considerable domestic opposition. That typically meant that the United States avoided pressures for democratization within its Middle Eastern allies, while encouraging instability and regime change where possible within Soviet clients. Iran was one of the earliest battlefields of the Cold War, as the United States (incorrectly) viewed the election of Prime Minister Mossadegh and his efforts toward nationalizing oil as part of a Soviet conspiracy and acted covertly to overturn his rule and return the Shah to the throne.

That constellation of interests largely defined the American view of the Middle East. In this conceptualization, Gulf connections to East Africa or to India didn't matter all that much, but the views of Gulf states toward Israel and Palestinian national movements mattered a great deal. Iran seemed a natural part of the region from this lens prior to the 1979 revolution, as it played a critical role in oil production and the nascent OPEC while fending off Soviet threats and serving as the primarily US military proxy in the Gulf region; after the revolution, Iran posed the most severe external threat to key American allies in the Gulf and Israel (by way of Lebanon's Hezbollah). From this perspective, Israel was part of the region by definition (even as it was excluded by the rest of the region), since much of US policy toward the region was intended to serve the interest of advancing Israeli security and the Palestinian issue lay at the heart of inter-Arab politics. Israel's role in cultivating African allies or supporting South African Apartheid – or its placement within the European group at the United Nations because of its political exclusion by the Arab bloc – did little to promote alternative conceptions of Israel as a transregional power (Gidron 2020).

The repeated Arab–Israeli wars played a key role in consolidating the full picture of the US conception of the Middle East as region. While the 1967 war gets the most attention as a transformational moment, the 1973 war arguably played a more critical role in consolidating a "regional" concept. In particular, the Saudi- and Iranian-led OPEC oil blockade in support of the Egyptian–Syrian attack of Israel established a connection between the Levant and the Gulf which would never really be forgotten. Washington's move to monopolize peace diplomacy after 1974 at the expense of the Soviet Union involved shuttle diplomacy not only to the frontline states and Israel, but also to Saudi Arabia and other regional stakeholders. Later, the peace process launched in 1991 explicitly came in response to the difficulties of maintaining alliance with both Israel and most of the Arab states; their participation in the coalition to liberate Kuwait had carried the cost of at least an effort to resolve the Israeli–Palestinian conflict. The Madrid peace process worked across dual tracks, one of them a series of bilateral negotiations between Israel and frontline Arab states and the other a multilateral track taking on issues of "regional" concern such as the environment and water – which affected but did not include a wider range of states than those considered part of the "Middle East."

The collapse of the Soviet Union and the crystallization of US primacy in the Middle East after 1991 perhaps surprisingly did not lead to any significant rethinking of regional boundaries. The Clinton administration remained focused on promoting Arab–Israeli peace, including the creation of a multilateral track in the Madrid peace talks which largely replicated membership in the Middle East, and the dual containment of Iran and Iraq, largely implemented through security cooperation with the Gulf states and Turkey. That agenda left little space for thinking beyond the traditional region. Middle East Studies too remained largely impervious to broader trends toward studies of globalization, democratization, and regional integration – in large part because none of those things which had become such popular objects of study in the discipline seemed to be happening within the region. The greater challenge in this era, as detailed next, was the turn toward global issues and the downgrading of all area studies within the academy and particularly within political science.

Stretching the Region from the Global War on Terror to the Arab Uprisings

The al-Qaeda attacks on 9/11 and the launch of the Global War on Terror which followed might have been a time for greater rethinking of regional concepts. After all, al-Qaeda had begun in Saudi Arabia and Egypt, launched its first attacks in Kenya and Tanzania, matured in Sudan, come of age in Afghanistan, and were ultimately harbored in Pakistan – all outside the traditional core Middle Eastern region. The battle against global jihadism extended from the start to Indonesia, the Philippines, and Somalia – even, by some metrics, to Bosnia and Chechnya to the north and to the Sahel in the south. The constellation of Al-Qaeda franchises – from AQAP and AQI to AQIM – and affiliates – from Shabab to the MILF – defied regional definition, as did al-Qaeda Central's fully globalized membership and networks. That more global battleground briefly led the Bush administration to advance a notion of the "broader Middle East" incorporating central Asia, but the new concept gained little traction either institutionally or in the public discourse. People still basically referred to the Middle East, and most academic institutions remained committed to existing regional definitions.

Declining US primacy has undermined concepts of the region rooted in American strategic priorities and institutional conventions. Those interested in "decolonizing" Middle East Studies have turned toward SWANA – Southwest Asia and North Africa – as an alternative to Western perspectives (Bishara 2023). This, the argument goes, rejects orienting geographically toward the West and instead positions the region in relation to Asia. While this shift has been popular among some constituencies, and reflects the general perception of rising Chinese and Russian power in the region, it has had few meaningful effects in terms of this Element's discussion. SWANA is no less positioned as a geographic unit than MENA or the Middle East before it, and if it includes a different set of countries, then this has not been consistently articulated in the literature. Nor has a compelling justification been offered for which countries to include. Indeed, beyond the rhetorical flourish of rejecting Western intellectual hegemony, it is difficult to see what SWANA changes at all.

The year 2011 brought the Arab regional identity to the fore, while the post-2013 collapse of those democratic transitions into regionalized wars accelerated the strategic integration of the non-Arab powers and gave more purchase to the Middle East regional concept (Lynch 2016, 2018). The diffusion of protest in 2011 followed a clearly identifiable pattern, spreading through Arab states while stopping at the linguistic and political boundaries. The collapse of many traditional Arab powers such as Egypt and Syria, following Iraq's destruction in 2003, invited a more active and influential role by strong, capable non-Arab states such as Israel, Iran, and Turkey – which proceeded to fight their battles increasingly on Arab soil in ways that brought the Middle East security concept to life in unprecedented ways even as most in the region rejected the identity proposals.

Whatever the strategic logic of grouping the Middle East from an historical globalist perspective, the new battlefields of the region simply do not respect the artificial lines on the map. Yemen's devastating war offers powerful testimony to the blurring of regional lines. The eruption of protests in 2011 placed Yemen very much within the Arab uprisings context, with its protest slogans and methods very closely mirroring the modalities of the rest of the regional wave. The American and regional response in the following several years similarly tracked with the typical Middle Eastern concept, with Washington largely acting through the Gulf Cooperation Council and Saudi Arabia to broker a transition agreement which would end the regime of Ali Abdullah Saleh without jeopardizing core regional interests. The Houthi takeover of Sanaa in 2014, as shocking a development as it was, still remained largely within the regional template. It did expand the scope, however, as observers inside (to some extent) and outside (to a greater extent) saw the rise of the Houthis as an Iranian gain within the regional struggle for power. The Saudi-led intervention in 2015 initially seemed to function in that register, as an unusual, but explicable, move within the Middle Eastern game of power politics. As the war dragged on, however, the Yemen war began to expand to incorporate the Red Sea and East African coast (Mabon and Mason 2022). The UAE in particular sought naval hegemony to enforce a blockade of weapons and resupply to the Houthis; that blockade failed to stem the growing flow of weapons and advisers from Iran, but it did serve as the justification for the consolidation of a maritime security architecture which spanned the two ostensibly discrete regions.

Other regional post-2011 conflicts followed a similar trajectory. Libya's war began as an uprising against the Qaddafi regime, and was shaped by an unprecedented joint Arab–NATO intervention. But Libya could not avoid having effects on and being affected by its Sahelian and Central African neighborhood. The collapse of the central state and division of the country into dueling blocs armed from the outside created a vacuum which attracted illicit flows of weapons, drugs, migrants, and more. Libya's war directly destabilized Chad and indirectly affected the trajectory of Mali, while also contributing to the rising tempo of conflict in the Darfur region of western Sudan. Libya, as noted earlier, was not at the time part of the US Central Command; that oversight has since been remedied. Qaddafi, the overthrown despot, also famously considered Libya to be as African as it was Arab, declaring himself the King of Kings and aggressively intervening in African politics. It is to such internal identity gambits and contentions that we now turn.

4 The Middle East from the Inside Out

Section 3 considered the ways in which external great powers defined and shaped the region around their interests. That story, however, is radically incomplete if it does not take into account the ways in which local elites and peoples imagined their region and acted politically within it. Hette's overview of the "new regionalism" literature acknowledged matter-of-factly that "there are no natural regions: definitions of a 'region' vary according to the particular problem or question under investigation. Moreover it is widely accepted that it is how political actors perceive and interpret the idea of a region and notions of regionness that is critical: all regions are socially constructed and hence politically contested" (Hettne 2015: 544). These local actors were never passive recipients of great power diktat, and continually worked to advance their local interests through both cooperation and conflict with those external powers. Beyond such power politics, there were significant economic and cultural processes unfolding over the course of decades which consolidated some concepts of region and undermined others. In general, it may make the most sense to view the Middle East as plausibly a region in geopolitical and security terms, but the Arab world more plausibly its own region in constructivist and ideational terms (Mabon 2020; Lynch and Mabon 2025). This has changed over time in critically interesting ways; in many ways the story of the decade since 2013 has been one of Israel, Iran, and Turkey each normalizing their inclusion in the region in distinctive – and controversial – ways.

There have been repeated attempts by regional powers and movements to define the region over the years, based on conceptions such as ethnicity, nationalism, religion, or proximity. Bilgin (2004) brings forth projects such as "the Arab world," "the Islamic world," and "Euro-Med" as examples of such projects. Some of these projects gained wide acceptance, while others remained either stillborn or attached to specific political projects. I distinguish between two types of identity projects in this section: those associated with states, either in competition over regional order or as attempted projections of power; and those built upon material foundations or transnational networks which have yet to fully manifest as potential regional identities. After reviewing both types, I conclude with a brief discussion of the interaction between inside-out and outside-in definitions of the Middle East as a region.

Alternative Identity Projects

There have been quite a few alternatives to the Middle East proposed from within the region, none of them yet successful in replacing it but each offering a different logic of regional construction. The extent to which these map onto local political identities and discourse, and inform patterns of political mobilization and contestation, can inform constructivist theoretical approaches to region.

"The Arab World"

The Arab world in many ways makes more sense as a "region" than the Middle East ever did. Unlike the Middle East, there are clearly demarcated boundaries based on language and ethnic identity, a shared community of fate rooted in core pan-Arab ideas such as support for Palestine and Arab unity, a shared public sphere, and a set of regional institutions (however moribund). The Arab world has, oddly, nonetheless largely been understood as an identity project and a form of political expression rather than as a world region. The limitations of the Arab world as a regional frame are worth exploring, as are the reasons why this definition has been contested and rejected both from inside and outside the region.

Arab nationalism, unlike any kind of Middle Eastern identity, has a long and rich history (Dawisha 2016). The demand for Arab unity is generally discussed as a natural outcome of the artificial creation of Arab states, which implicitly frustrated an existing demand for a unified Arab-wide political order. But, as Malcolm Kerr famously demonstrated, such a clear demand for unity did not manifest as cooperative politics even at (or, more accurately, especially during) the height of the so-called Arab Cold War (Kerr 1965; Barnett 1998). What pan-Arabism did do, however, is to define the common stakes of Arab political order, establishing a clear hierarchy of shared concerns, passions, and discourses which constituted Arab identity within a shared Arab language public sphere (Lynch 2006). Pan-Arabism could not offer a single answer about how to support Palestine, but it demanded that all actors justify their behavior in terms of supporting Palestine (Barnett 1998; Lynch 2006). Pan-Arabism justified transnational interventionism, from Nasser's calls for popular uprisings in Lebanon and Jordan to Baathist Party organizations spanning the Levant to direct Egyptian and Saudi military intervention in Yemen or even Iraq's 1990 invasion of Kuwait, but it also could be made to justify the Arab participation in the coalition to liberate Kuwait from Iraq and Arab collective policies based on respect for state sovereignty. In other words, pan-Arabism defined the normatively appropriate arenas for competition and intervention and served as an authentic, widely shared, and even taken-for-granted regional concept for most of the people living in the region while remaining quite malleable in terms of its substantive content.

Pan-Arabism was not only ideational, however. There were material foundations for an Arab region as well, even if they were often overlooked because they did not involve European style increases in trade or formal customs unions. Perhaps the most important of the material foundations was the large-scale labor migration of Arabs from North Africa and the Levant to build the rapidly developing wealthy Gulf states. Jordanians, Egyptians, Palestinians, and other Arabs took on leading roles across most sectors in the rapidly transforming Gulf – from construction and civil engineering to education and culture. The linguistic unity mattered a great deal here, as Levantine and Egyptian Arabs could step smoothly into state bureaucracies or public school classrooms in ways which North Africans – to say nothing of Kurds, Persians, or other non-Arabs – could not.

Through this labor migration, generations of Arabs of all social classes gained firsthand knowledge of the Gulf states, while also interacting with each other on a regular basis. It is in these communities where we see the emergence of the Palestinian National Movement; Yasir Arafat and Fatah came together in Kuwait and were able to fundraise effectively across the Gulf for the struggle for Palestine. It is also in the interaction between Egyptian-style Muslim Brothers and Saudi-style Wahhabism that new strands of radical jihadism came together to produce the explosive growth of Salafism in Egypt and elsewhere in the region and laid the foundations for violent jihadist movements in countries such as Algeria. In 1990, most Arab states joined the US-led coalition against Iraq in the name of liberating Kuwait, despite widespread mass sympathy for Iraqi complaints and enthusiasm for the principle of Arab unification. The expulsion of vast numbers of Arabs from the Gulf states out of anger over their support for Saddam or fear for their potential political loyalties shattered one of the key material dimensions of regional unification, while their replacement with primarily South Asians helped to build the foundations for new forms of subregional and transregional connectivity.

This pan-Arab definition only went so far, of course. The Arab world involved the Kurds, spanning Turkey, Iraq, Iran, and Syria. Morocco and Algeria battled over the Western Sahara despite its irrelevance to broader pan-Arab concerns. Libya under Qaddafi intervened in African as well as Middle Eastern arenas with gusto. But it's also worth placing the rise of pan-Arabism in the context of other possible conceptualizations: specifically, the appeal of the Global South framework and potential resonances with pan-Africanism. Pan-Arabism, by delimiting the scope of shared political identity and interventionism, had the effect of carving "the Middle East" off from global anti-colonial struggles. This was not perfectly achieved, of course: China backed the Dhofar Rebellion in Oman (Takriti 2013), while Soviet interventionism in Afghanistan impacted politics in the Gulf. But overall, it is remarkable how fully the focus on Palestine and pan-Arabism over more global revolutionary causes served to sever potential connections with African and Asian liberation movements.

The Arab core of the Middle East defined itself in part against the three major non-Arab players, each of which became increasingly powerful and central to regional dynamics over time and each of which faced distinctive challenges rooted in identity and inclusion. Israel, of course, was negatively defined, excluded from regional order by virtue of its occupation of Palestine. This, arguably, explains better than anything else the reasons why the Arab world conception was rejected by the international community and by the United States: boycotting and excluding Israel was seen as a political project to be rejected, which meant that a "region" which defined itself in those terms could not pass muster within academic area studies demarcated in large part by US interests and funding. No Middle East Studies Center could be allowed to teach Arabic but not Hebrew (other regional languages such as Persian, Turkish, and Kurdish tended to be more optional). Why "the Arab world" was viewed as a political project and "the Middle East" as a neutral, objective descriptor for a world region should continue to be interrogated even as those understandings were largely naturalized within the academy.

Pan-Arabism lost its luster in the 1970s, though (Ajami 1978, 1992). The crushing defeat by Israel in 1967, followed in short order by the death of Gamal Abdel Nasser and the brutal crushing of the PLO by Jordan's Arab Legion, left an ideological void. The 1973 war proved far more successful, with careful strategic coordination between Egypt and Syria backed by Saudi Arabia's oil weapon, but was manifestly fought in the name of state self-interest and featured little of the ideological fireworks of the 1960s. The following years saw the shift of power toward the newly wealthy Gulf and the consolidation of overwhelming national security states optimized to smother any manifestation of public opposition. In that heavily securitized environment, Arab states cooperated against Iran and ostracized Egypt after Camp David, but otherwise did little in the name of Arab cooperation. Israel invaded Lebanon, leaving behind a devastating eight year civil war as the PLO fled to distant Tunisia, with little effective Arab pushback.

But the Arab world concept did not fade away, despite the expectations (and hopes) of many observers inside and out. Saddam Hussein tried, with more success than was acknowledged at the time, to rally popular pan-Arab sentiment against the US-led liberation of Kuwait in 1990–91. Arabist narratives about the region found a voice with Qatar's 1996 launch of the satellite television station al-Jazeera, which won a vast audience through professional news coverage framed within a pan-Arab lens and rambunctious talk shows openly arguing about the most contentious issues in public life (Lynch 2006). Al-Jazeera helped to crystallize new popular conceptions of the region through its choices of what to cover and how to cover it. Tunisia's 2010 uprising became a pan-Arab issue rather than a local one in no small part because of how al-Jazeera framed its coverage – and al-Jazeera's enthusiastic embrace of the Arab Spring helped to shape the bounds and intensity of the diffusion of protest across the Arab world. It's interesting in this regard that Iran's 2009 Green Movement protests and Turkey's 2013 Gezi Park protests objectively appear similar to the Arab uprisings, but were not understood that way by either the participants or by Arab observers, and sparked no comparable imitation or diffusion. The heavy focus by al-Jazeera on Palestine – starting with its groundbreaking coverage of the second Intifada which arguably launched it to its dominant position in the Arab media – had the unexpected effect of legitimating Israel as part of the region in ways that Iran and Turkey were not. But that inclusion in the region did not transfer into support for normalization with Israel among Arab viewers – quite the opposite.

Israel and "The New Middle East," the Mosaic, and the Periphery Strategy

Israel had its own mental maps of the region which served its core interests. It from the outset pursued what has been called a periphery strategy and offered a "mosaic" conceptualization of the region's nature. In this approach, the primary obstacle to Israeli security and ambitions lay in the distinctly and uniquely Arab support for Palestine and hostility to the Zionist project. Israel therefore looked to circumvent that Arab opposition by reaching out to minority groups which might feel dominated by the hegemony of Arabism: Kurds, Amazigh, Jews, Christians, and so forth. It also looked to form alliances with non-Arab states on the periphery of the Middle East, such as Turkey and Iran, as well as beyond the boundaries of the region (for instance, in sub-Saharan Africa and Central Asia) (Alpher 2015; Gidron 2020). A conception of the region in which Arabs and Jews were only parts of a complex mosaic of ethnicities and religions would have the effect of breaking apart the bipolar, monolithic conflict between Israel and the Arab world while opening up opportunities for destabilizing rival regional states.

During the peace process which began in Madrid in 1991, and especially after the 1993 Oslo Accords, Israel began to normalize in critical ways, both through indirect cooperation with Arab states and through the direct participation in forums such as the multilateral component of the Madrid process. It is worth reflecting here on why "normalization" was so important in this context. Israel had cooperated with states such as the UAE against Iran long before the Abraham Accords. It had representation in many Gulf capitals. Normalization offered no additional security, and its absence would not have stood in the way of the trade benefits which the UAE and Israel trumpeted following the signature. And yet Israel has long placed a high value on normalization (Sela 1998).

Both of its peace treaties, with Jordan and Egypt, had delivered major strategic and security benefits but had ended in a "cold peace" where public opinion continued to firmly reject Israel's legitimacy and to support Palestinians against its occupation and repeated military assaults on Gaza. The security it sought was what IR theorists have called ontological security, a desire for recognition and a fit between self-image and treatment by others (Mitzen 2006; Bianco 2024). In essence, Israel wanted to be part of the Middle East, recognized by others as a legitimate and normal part of the terrain, its "right to exist" no longer questioned. Right-wing Israelis, of course, placed less stock in such acceptance; they believed that recognition would come through power and that the other states of the region would value that power regardless of their treatment of Palestinians.

The hope for a "new Middle East" has been a persistent feature of political discourse about regional order. This discourse connotes a region in which the Palestinian issue had declined in salience, Realpolitik dominated over identity politics, and oppressive states effectively prevented any public pressure for policy change. It first rose to prominence in the early 1990s, in line with the Oslo peace process. In those years, Shimon Peres floated the idea of a "new Middle East" based – unironically – on the marriage of Jewish brains, Gulf capital, and Arab labor. A set of Egyptian, Jordanian, and other Arab intellectuals briefly joined forces with Israeli peace advocates in the so-called "Copenhagen Group" convened to flesh out this new Middle East; most were shunned in their home countries after their participation was exposed, and the whole thing faded away as the peace process stalled. The idea of Arab cooperation with Israel returned, however, based on the shared perception of threat from Iran and by American encouragement. In 2006, key Arab states such as Saudi Arabia initially sided with Israel in its war on Lebanon, blaming Hezbollah rather than Israel for the provocation; US Secretary of State Condoleezza Rice famously described it as "the birth pangs of a new Middle East." In 2020, the UAE, along with Bahrain, and Morocco, signed the so-called Abraham Accords which normalized relations with Israel without reference to the Palestinian issue. And in 2023, the United States pushed hard to bring about Saudi–Israeli normalization along with promoting a broader new infrastructure for intra-regional trade and cooperation.

But each time, that regional order proved unsustainable. The Oslo peace process failed, giving way to the bloody second Intifada. Arab support for Israel against Hezbollah in 2006 barely lasted a few weeks before public opinion forced them to reverse course. And the Abraham Accords and the Biden push for regional reordering were soon overshadowed and delegitimated by the October 7 Hamas attack on Israel and the subsequent Israeli destruction of

Gaza. Why did each effort to promote a political project of a new Middle East fail so dramatically? One answer is the broad public opposition to normalization with Israel, which the regional conception defined by Arab identity offered by al-Jazeera fostered and supported. The Abraham Accords tended to be embraced by the most authoritarian regimes which could afford to ignore public opinion completely (the UAE and Bahrain); the most desperate, which would do anything for international assistance (Sudan); or the most canny, who were happy to trade intangible words for concrete recognition of their core issues (Morocco) (Fakhro 2024). None of that translated into a broadly accepted conception of the natural region which included Israel as a normal, accepted component. Israel's place in the Middle East after the Abraham Accords, especially during its war on Gaza, offers a critical test of the realist and constructivist approaches to region.

Iran: "Resistance"

Iran, after the 1979 Islamic revolution, was defined by opposition to the regional and international orders. Its counter-hegemonic struggle against the United States and its regional allies was legitimated by multiple different potential identity projects which might link together the disparate countries of the region. The most immediately available, pan-Shi'ism, was both potent and problematic. The pan-Shi'ite model could draw on a long history of transnational Shi'a clerical networks and find points of access in well-established Shi'a communities across not only the Gulf and Iraq but also across Afghanistan and Pakistan and the broader Persianate world of Central Asia. It had marginal success in the immediate revolutionary period, as Arab regimes terrified of the spread of revolution cracked down hard on any sign of mobilization in Shi'a communities (Matthiesen 2023). During the 1980s, its efforts to spread revolution triggered balancing coalitions such as the 1981 formation of the Gulf Cooperation Council as well as Iraq's 1980 invasion backed by frightened Gulf states (Gause 2009).

The model of exporting revolution faded over the course of the 1980s, and ultimately gave way to a more enduring alternative model of the Middle East: Resistance. This identity project accepted in broad terms the idea that the region had been defined by Western imperialism, and sought to position Iran as the leader of those peoples – which it believed to be the vast majority – which rejected that neocolonial framework. Resistance as an identity was carefully tailored to avoid sectarian connotations, with Shi'ism given a back seat compared with a much more broadly appealing narrative of countering American and Zionist domination. Arab states, especially Saudi Arabia, responded in part by trying to highlight Iran's Shi'a and Persian roots as a way of discrediting its broadly popular identity project (Mabon 2020).

After the US invasion of Iraq in 2003, Iran moved increasingly openly and forcefully into the heartland of the Middle East, rendering moot any questions about its inclusion in the region. Iranian allies held power in Lebanon, Syria, Iraq, and eventually Yemen – a zone of influence which Jordan's King Abdullah infamously described as a "Shia crescent aimed at the heart of the Arab world." Iran viewed its presence differently, of course, presenting itself as the core of the "Axis of Resistance" to Israel, the United States, and their Arab allies alike. It attempted to downplay its Shi'ism in favor of Resistance discourse, appealing with some success to an Arab public opinion consistently at odds with the policies of their governments (as in 2006, when Sunni Islamist movements and broader Arab public opinion rallied in support of Shi'a Hezbollah during Israel's war on Lebanon). Those governments in turn sought to isolate Iran by highlighting its Shi'ism and Persian identity, while aligning strategically with Israel in ways which accelerated both Israel's incorporation into the Middle East and Iran's appeal to outraged publics. This evolved after 2011, as Iran's role became both more prominent and more controversial with various Arab audiences and actors. Iran used Shi'a identity instrumentally building powerful militias to fight on the side of Bashar al-Asad in Syria and to leverage a dominant role in Iraq; its relationship with Yemen's Houthi movement was more alliance than patron-proxy, but similarly provocative in the region.

Turkey: Neo-Ottomanism Meets Islamism

Turkey occupied an uneasy place in the Middle East, an ambiguity reflected in its internal political cultural debates and foreign policy discourses (Hintz 2019). Arab nationalism had, of course, initially begun as a revolt against the Turkish domination in the late Ottoman Empire. Turkey had long sought to turn its back on its Middle Eastern identity in favor of pursuing integration into the West via NATO and even the European Union. But in the 1990s, Erdogan's AKP invented a neo-Ottoman identity hearkening back to past Turkish presence in the Arab regions which could translate into greater inclusion and influence in the Middle East. Under the rubric of "no problems with neighbors," Ankara built relations with Syria while casting about for Arab support by vocally attacking Israel and distributing popular television soap operas. Unlike Iran, Turkey had few Turkic ethnic communities to draw upon in its efforts to spread influence (except in parts of Iraq). And whatever political purpose the neo-Ottoman project provided inside of Turkey, no part of the Middle East in fact yearned for an Ottoman restoration or even to be reminded of their historical subordination. It is telling that Turkey instead cultivated Islamist networks such as the Muslim Brotherhood rather than seriously advancing an alternative to the Middle East grounded in the glorious and far-reaching Ottoman past.

Turkey pursued both regional and extra-regional ambitions in the post-2011 period, complicating its identification with the Middle East as region. While its ambitions to join Europe receded, Turkey intervened ever more aggressively in the Caucasus and in Africa in part through the export of its indigenous drone production. Turkey engaged broadly across Africa, opening hundreds of *diwaniyat* religious institutions to spread its cultural influence (Donelli 2021). It also intervened directly in Libya, helping its Islamist allies in western Libya push back the advances of the UAE-Egyptian-backed Libyan National Army and stabilize a long-term ceasefire. It backed Qatar forcefully during the 2017 blockade led by Saudi Arabia and the UAE, only to later reconcile with its adversaries and move back into the center of regional politics.

The Islamic World: Non-State Regional Identity Projects

To this point, we have focused on identity projects associated with states (Israel, Iran, and Turkey) or appropriated by states in pursuit of power and regional leadership (pan-Arabism). There are other ways to think about the Middle East as a region defined from within that are not reducible to state power projects. The most important of these, and the most potentially radical when taken to its logical conclusion, is the concept of the Islamic world. There are as many different competing visions and projects associated with the Islamic world as there were in the Arab world. They involve radically different conceptions of order, authority, and inclusion, and position themselves quite differently against or with the broader global system. If viewed through the contemporary state system, the Islamic world concept would force an expansion of the analytical lens far beyond the "Middle East" to include the vast Muslim populations of India, Pakistan, Indonesia, Nigeria, and beyond. For all the occasional activity of the Organization of Islamic Countries (OIC) or the Muslim World League (MWL), there is no serious analytical trend or political project which presents the Islamic world as a coherent region for comparative analysis (a problem to which we return in Section 5).

Saudi Arabia offers a useful window into these complexities. For all of its centrality to the politics of the Middle East, it consistently viewed itself as central to global Islam and acted accordingly. The spread of Saudi Wahhabist doctrines of Islam happened through large-scale financial investments, the organizational muscle of the Muslim World League, and the soft power appeal of the Islamic University of Medina, which attracted countless of the best and brightest young Islamic scholars from across Africa and Asia as well as the Middle East (Farquhar 2016). This transnational and reactionary project of religious and social transformation across the globe challenged both regional divides and the state system. In practice, however, Saudi Arabia served as a key node in the American imperium and sought leadership within the Middle Eastern region, which neutered the potentially transformative nature of its political vision.

On the opposite extreme, al-Qaeda, the Islamic State, and other Salafi-jihadist movements offer a radical rejection of the core institutions and conceptual foundations of international relations. That includes the idea of a "Middle East" somehow distinct from the rest of the world. In the jihadist worldview, the world is divided not by region – or by race, nationality, ethnicity, or any other ascriptive characteristic. The meaningful divide is between Islam and others – Dar al-Islam and Dar al-Harb – and the Muslim community (the umma) is to be found wherever Muslims live. In the conception of jihad developed over the course of the 1980s and 1990s by thinkers such as Abdullah Azzam (Hegghammer 2020) and put into practice by al-Qaeda and others, the religious obligation to fight on behalf of Muslims under occupation or threat was truly global. The fighters of the jihad should view the suffering of Muslims in Chechnya, Bosnia, the Philippines, or the Sahel no differently than they should those of Palestine or the Arabian Peninsula. In such a world, the Middle East should carry no weight as a region, even if local battles might be made to resonate with broader regional conflicts and narratives (as with Abu Musab al-Zarqawi's harnessing of Sunni–Shi'a tensions in his Iraqi jihad).

Somewhere in the middle, the Muslim Brotherhood represents a transnational organization which is primarily Middle Eastern but has genuinely global reach which largely accommodated itself to the nation-state system. The Muslim Brotherhood originated in Egypt in 1928 and quickly spread to establish branches across the Middle East. Labor migration to the Gulf and Palestinian dispossession by Israel equally assisted this regionalization of the Brotherhood. Brotherhood members fleeing Nasserist repression in the 1950s staffed the newly created Saudi and Gulf education ministries and schools (Lacroix 2014). It's interesting here, again, how little synergistic interaction really took place between the Brotherhood and the largely contemporaneous Islamist movements emerging in Pakistan; Mawdudi's ideas were not far from Banna's or Qutb's, but never entered the Islamist canon in the same way. But Islamism in its Muslim Brotherhood variants emerged as a key transnational movement connecting political trends across the region. Every Muslim Brotherhood national branch retained its independence, with each evolving in response to its own local conditions. Jordan's Muslim Brotherhood became a pillar of regime support for decades, buttressing the monarchy against the PLO and liberalizing demands from Palestinian-origin citizens. Qatar's Muslim Brotherhood largely dissolved into the state after thoroughly colonizing state bureaucracies. Tunisia's Ennahda suffered extreme repression upon its emergence and was forced underground or into exile before re-emerging after 2011. Algeria's Muslim Brotherhood equivalent aligned with Salafis in the ill-fated Islamic Salvation Front in 1991, where it was poised to sweep elections before a military coup ended democracy and unleashed decades of brutal civil war.

Despite these disparate experiences, these Muslim Brotherhood organizations typically shared common intellectual references, organizational structures, and political orientations. Their mutual support for each other ensured that national politics became regional concerns, while their shared support for Hamas, which emerged out of the Jordanian/Palestinian Muslim Brotherhood, centered a common regional agenda. Part of that shared regional agenda was the struggle for democratic openings, where Muslim Brotherhood organizations emerged as primary opposition parties in elections held in Algeria, Egypt, Jordan, Tunisia, and Yemen. And, above all, Palestine united them as a core political, religious, and normative commitment in ways which marked them as distinctly Middle Eastern.

Subregional Possibilities

The Middle East has long seen subregional projects advancing the internal coherence of distinct historical and geographic regions. The Maghreb states have much in common, from deep history to French colonialism to the transnational Amazigh presence and connections to the Sahel; in the 1980s, the so-called "Mashreq-Maghreb Debate" opened up important discussions about comparative state formation and the substantive meaning of Arab unity. The Levant has distinctive patterns and structures rooted in Ottoman legacies that make any part of it deeply familiar to anyone from another part – save, perhaps, for the colonized and transformed Israeli parts of Palestine. The early days of the Arab order, states, and public figures competed to advance related political projects to unite the Levant under concepts such as Greater Syria, a unified Arab Kingdom under Hashemite rule, or the Fertile Crescent project; as Kerr so brutally documented, these usually fell apart amid the self-interest of the competing state actors.

The Maghreb has a strong claim toward subregional identity. It shares characteristics that it does not share with the rest of the so-called Middle East, characteristics that plausibly have distinctive political implications. The Maghreb countries are Francophone, and their state institutions were all profoundly shaped by the same French colonial institutions, the same French obsessions with secularism, the same French racism. They all have an Amazigh minority for long years were politically suppressed and culturally ignored. And materially, they all have sent vast numbers of economic migrants to Europe rather than the Gulf, where they established their own subcommunities and transnational networks of migration and economic exchange. Morocco has been particularly keen to develop a role in the Sahel and French West Africa through the promotion of religious institutions, while it competes intensely with Algeria over control of the Western Sahara (in 2020, Morocco normalized relations with Israel to win American support for its claims, illustrating the ongoing regional interactions). For all of the Maghreb's commonality and its orientations south to the Sahel and north to Europe, its connections to the Middle East remain potent.

The Gulf too has a strong claim toward subregional identity. The Arabian Peninsula states have a great deal in common, from tribal structures and monarchies to oil wealth and the demand for migrant labor. The GCC has gone further than any other Arab regional organization in promoting functional integration (or at least it had before the UAE, Saudi Arabia, and Bahrain announced a blockade of Qatar in 2017). In recent years, there has been a growing push for recognizing the Gulf as a distinct and coherent political region (often with triumphalist undertones) – even as a critical literature has pushed against Gulf exceptionalism and argued for viewing it in conventional comparative terms. But even as the Gulf objectively differentiated from the rest of the Middle East in the 2010s and became increasingly active in Africa and in global forums, it simultaneously became far more directly and intensely involved in inter-Arab politics than ever before (Hanieh 2018).

Overall, then, subregional projects look more like identifiable regions than does the Middle East as a whole, with more shared history and culture and more intense interactions. But subregion ultimately cannot account for their embeddedness within broader regional political battles and the pressures of geopolitics toward regional behavior.

It is intriguing to then compare those subregional projects with some which have all the historical foundations and material realities of a subregion but which have for the most part not crystallized as an identity or a project. First, the *western Indian Ocean*. The connections between the Arabian Peninsula and the Horn of Africa were long and deep: Oman long ruled Zanzibar, Swahili is spoken across many of the cities of the Gulf, slavery brought countless East Africans through Gulf ports, the dhow trade long connected economies, culture, and society. In recent years, the UAE, Qatar, Turkey, Egypt, and Iran have vied for influence in the Horn, building alliances, purchasing farmland, securing port access. The UAE, in particular, has pursued a maritime strategy connecting the

Horn to the Gulf through Yemen as part of its broader regional ambition (Mabon and Mason 2022). This all makes for the stuff of transregional analysis: "the Indian Ocean makes visible a range of lateral networks that fall within the Third World or Global South. It is hence of particular relevance to those pursuing post–area studies scholarship" (Hofmeyr 2012: 584) And yet that transregion has largely failed to get traction outside of small corners of the academy – and routinely falls ignored between different area studies centers.

Second, the *Mediterranean*. The traditional area studies model "rendered the Mediterranean all but invisible" (Watkins 2013) despite a long history of deep interconnectivity. The Euro-Med initiative was launched by the European Union with the North African states in November 1995 via the Barcelona Declaration to find ways to navigate trade and labor migration issues within the context of accelerating European integration (Adler et al., 2016; Del Sarto 2020). Here, the material foundations were strong, particularly the large and entrenched communities of North African workers in European countries bound to their homelands by dense webs of financial remittances, ongoing communications, and regular travel. There was also a historical foundation to build upon, given the long history of the Mediterranean as a cultural unit (Green 2014). The Euro-Med project arguably failed, however, because of its nakedly strategic motivations and the starkly racist underpinnings of unequal exchange between Europe and North Africa. North Africans had little reason to buy into a regional concept built around managing the problems which they were considered to have created, no matter what material benefits might flow from the official partnerships. Nor did the proposal of a shared Mediterranean civilization overcome the divides between the Maghreb and the Levantine countries, Turkey, or Egypt – or overcome the thorny problem of Israel's place along the Mediterranean coast.

Identity and Regions

Buzan and Waever make very clear in *Regions and Powers* that the self-perception of states and people makes no analytical difference; what matters to them is what states do, not what people feel. That aligns with much of the outside-in analysis of international relations. But this will not do. This section has argued that it must matter that there has never been a successful regional identity project based on "the Middle East," and that those which do advance that frame have been resoundingly rejected either by popular resistance or by powerful regional actors. To the extent that regimes formulate their foreign policy based on their perceptions of threat and the demands of symbolic competition, their understandings of the region in which they operate must matter to some degree. And to the degree that public opinion is able to impose itself on the regime security obsession of regimes, it would seem to matter that those publics overwhelmingly seem to prefer Arab or Islamic regional concepts. It is here, in the domain of identity, norms, discourse, and shared understandings, that area studies approaches offer essential insights into the nature of regions which resonate with constructivist approaches in the broader IR literature.

5 The Middle East and Comparative Area Studies

The problematic nature of the Middle East as a region has not, contrary to popular belief, been fatal for the political science of the region. After generations of self-flagellation over the failure of Middle East Studies to contribute to the core of mainstream political science, the field has actually made great advances and regularly engages with the field (Lynch, Schwedler, and Yom 2022). The purpose of this Element is not to criticize Middle East Studies or to call for it to be abandoned. Quite the contrary: the currently strong standing of Middle East area studies within the discipline offers a prime opportunity to expand and extend in innovative directions. In this final section, I reflect on the evolution, contestation, and alternative visions of the Middle East as a region and then offer a set of suggestions for how this might inform the subfield's approach to research and teaching in the coming years.

The previous two sections have explored how the "Middle East" was constructed and shaped by external powers and by local regional players and processes. But how does all of that matter for political science? Is it simply an historical curiosity which can then be safely moved past, or does it actually impact the practice of political science research? In this section, I argue that there has been an overwhelming regional insularity in Middle East political science, with Middle Eastern states almost exclusively compared with each other and with large-n quantitative studies overwhelmingly adopting the region as the universe of cases. This would be fine, if there were in fact reliable justifications for grouping those cases together. But if the definition of region is arbitrary or political, then much of what political science thinks it knows about the Middle East may be an artifact of a truncated universe of cases (Smith and Waldner 2021).

My argument in this section is a bit different from that which stoked the "area studies controversy," that perennial debate about the relative value of close studies of countries and regions compared with developing universalizable theories. Here, I tend to side with those who note that scholars well grounded in specific cases and regions tend to produce theories at least as robust as, and probably more robust, than those who lack empirical knowledge about the world they claim to describe. But for the purposes of this Element, the distinction is largely irrelevant: the question at issue is not whether area studies is productive, but rather what counts as the area to be studied.

As discussed in Section 2, the area studies controversy has been a recurrent discourse within political science, taking different forms but largely repeating the same debates. This tension emerged in tandem with the move toward the professionalization of political science as a "science" in the 1960s, with behavioralists pushing the discipline toward quantification, formalization, and general theory. Modernization theory loomed large in that trend – and Middle Eastern cases such as Turkey and Egypt loomed large in the core texts of modernization theory (Rustow, Lerner, etc.). The rise of rational choice theory in the 1980s laid the foundation for the early 1990s assault on area knowledge aimed at relegating it to the subordinate role of providing examples and data to higher-order theorists (and also at appropriating the institutional and financial resources which had heretofore protected area studies centers from their departments), as Bates (1997) acknowledges frankly in his widely cited short article on area studies.

The end of the Cold War and the rise of globalization as the dominant political and theoretical narrative in the early 1990s drove a wholesale rethinking of the area studies across many of the major foundations and funding organizations had an equally dramatic effect on Middle East Studies (Hajjar and Niva 1997). The area studies went out of fashion, as academic and funding trends drifted toward global themes and universalizing grand theories. The SSRC's decision in the 1990s to eliminate area studies programs in favor of global and functional programs sparked wide-ranging albeit inconclusive discussion of the value of the area studies. In practice, however, the institutional framework of area studies largely survived the shifts in foundation fashion. Few, if any, university-based area studies centers shifted their names or missions, the regional studies associations such as MESA continued with business as usual, and scholars continued to publish based on their well-cultivated expertise and professional networks.

That is not to say that nothing changed, however. Within political science more than other disciplines, the shift in funding priorities coincided with the widespread adoption of the Keohane/King/Verba model of causal inquiry which implicitly or explicitly relegated the area studies to sources of empirical material for the pursuit of general theory. For publications in the highest-ranked disciplinary journals, and for many of the most influential books, non-Western countries in Africa, the Middle East, and the rest of the global South became something like laboratories for the application and testing of general theories rather than cases to be appreciated fully in their own right. In place of hard-earned area expertise, it became remarkably common for successful Western researchers to parachute in for a few days to carry out surveys – or even just to train local scholars to do the surveys – and perhaps have a fixer set up a few interviews, and then publish articles without ever really engaging with the history, culture, people, or local politics of the country ostensibly being studied. The studies of democratic participation, ethnic politics, or experimental survey framing which followed largely abstracted from local political concerns or particularities in favor of explanatory rigor and causal identification strategies (Wedeen 2016; Teti and Abbott 2023). International relations theory became in the 2000s a key vehicle for yet another iteration of the area studies controversy (Teti 2007; Valbjørn 2023; Aris 2020; Bank and Busse 2021).

Much of the angst that this produced within Middle East political science centered around the difficulties which area experts faced with publishing in top disciplinary journals, a recurrent concern over the decades. That has given way in recent years, particularly since the 2011 Arab uprisings, to an unmistakable upsurge in political science of the Middle East appearing across the premiere outlets of the discipline (Berlin and Syed 2022; Cammett and Kendall 2022; Lynch, Schwedler, and Yom 2022). The Arab uprisings generated research puzzles of broad interest across political science: the causes of protest diffusion; the variation in regime stability in the face of mass protest; civil–military relations; social media effects; proxy warfare and new forms of intervention; and more. This has facilitated not only a much greater volume of publications about the Middle East in disciplinary journals but also much more prevalent citations of area studies knowledge in disciplinary research.

Teti and Abbott (2023) argue that the recent success of Middle East political science has largely been achieved by squeezing out its life and substance, substituting quantification for area studies knowledge. Something similar has been observed in African Studies, where influential publications and research trends have been accused of treating the continent like a laboratory for running controlled experiments to test pre-registered hypotheses rather than as a legitimate object of study in its own right. A disproportionate percentage of MENA publications in top political science journals in recent years have relied upon survey experiments, social media big data analysis, and statistical analysis of existing opinion surveys or datasets rather than field research. But there have also been enough remark-ably innovative articles and books based on deep field research and novel methodological approaches – often published in the top disciplinary jour-nals – to take such critique with a grain of salt. The closing of more and more of the region to researchers due to war or repression by autocratic regimes may push more scholars toward such research from a distance, whether we like it or not. Still, I find their critique is overblown, reaching its dire conclusions by adopting an implausibly rigid definition of what counts as "comparative." While there have been a healthy range of "laboratory" publications in the mix, the majority of these post-2011 publications were grounded in the extended fieldwork, language expertise, and attention to local particularities which are the hallmark of the best area studies.

But I am less interested here in the subfield's success in moving beyond the area studies controversy than in the ongoing problem of comparative area studies: even the efflorescence of the last decade has retained a general regional insularity, for the most part, which matched the seeming containment of the uprisings within the "Arab world" context. Why did we all accept the framing of Tunisia's 2010/2011 revolution as the first of the Arab uprisings rather than placing it within the prior decade of activism and uprisings across Africa (Branch and Mampilly 2015)? Why was Syria's post-2011 war compared to Iraq's post-2003 war but rarely to the long-running, deeply internationalized, and quite comparable wars in Afghanistan or Congo? Why was the failure of democratization theorized by reference to systematic failure across the Arab domains rather than to the mixed patterns of success and failure across comparable cases in Africa and Central Asia? Why do we compare Arab oil-producing rentier states and not all oil-producing rentier states (Smith and Waldner 2021)?

It is difficult to not conclude that the Middle East literature, despite its remarkable progress across other domains, is plagued by insularity shaped by the internalization and institutionalization of the definition of region. The vast majority of comparative work on the Middle East – whether case study based or large-n statistical work – still typically takes the unproblematized region as an enclosed comparative universe. The tendency to focus only on MENA cases as a self-enclosed universe fits with longer running patterns in Middle East political science. Mark Berlin and Anum Pasha Syed (2022) reviewed 283 Middle East focused articles appearing in nine major political science journals between 1990 and 2019. They found that "cross-regional scholarship . . . appears limited and primarily focuses on comparison with states in North America and Western Europe." They found that while 26.5% of the articles included a comparison to a non-MENA case, only 18% of those were to African cases, 12.6% to Latin American cases, and 13.5% to South Asian cases. The key point here, of course, is that even the best post–Arab uprisings scholarship loses a bit of its purchase if the Middle East is not a "region" defined by unique and identifiable differences. And that brings us to comparative area studies.

Comparative Area Studies

Perhaps the greatest problem posed by the difficulty of defining regions in world politics comes not from the study of politics within a particular region or country but rather from the attempt to implicitly or explicitly compare regions (Ahram 2011). There are different ways of mobilizing regions in comparative analysis, of course. Basedau and Koller (2007) offer a useful distinction between inter-regional (how broad global trends affect different regions), intra-regional, and cross-regional comparison. Intra-regional comparison assumes that countries within a region share enough in common to justify comparison, presumably by holding factors such as geography, climate, or culture constant. Inter-regional and cross-regional comparison both assume that regions have enough internal coherence that it makes sense to use them as units of analysis when evaluating the effects of global processes. Hanson usefully quotes Harry Eckstein on the point that regions/areas are only justifiable if "the societies and polities of different regions constitute distinctive types" (Hanson 2009). This Element has argued that those assumptions are at best problematic, but the literature has largely proceeded as if they were not.

Comparing across regions is one of those things which seems obvious in theory but becomes problematic in practice. There is always implicit comparison, of course; think about Toqueville holding France in his mind as he contemplated America. Much of early political science (especially but not only modernization theory) implicitly relied on European or American history as the template of normality, with areas in some sense defined by their deviance from those (very different) trajectories. Thus, the absence of democracy becomes a puzzle to be explained by virtue of the lack of something to be found in the West or the persistence of tribalism becomes a puzzle by virtue of the fading of such loyalties in the West. The study of regional international relations in the 1960s often proceeded in a similar way, seeking to identify reasons why areas of the world did not behave in the ways that European-generated theory predicted that they should. Such comparison is not only appropriate, but essential to the political science mission; Solingen's (2007) comparison of democratization in Latin America, Asia, and the Middle East offers an excellent positive example of such regional comparison.

The problem arises with the shift from comparison *across* regions to comparison *of* regions, when the level of analysis is taken to be the region – an arbitrary grouping which is assumed to share fundamental attributes – rather than individual countries or clearly comparable sets of countries. Seeking to understand the difference in economic development between Egypt and Brazil is one thing; examining the divergence between "the Middle East" and "Latin

America" is quite another. Ahram (2011) offers an excellent overview of methodological issues which arise, particularly the (mis)use of regional dummy variables in quantitative analysis, typically without explicit discussion or justification of the membership of the region in question.

It is worth repeating here that this is not necessarily about the traditional area studies debate, the methodological debate over whether politics is best understood through a close study rooted in field research and language skills or through more universalizable formal models. Intra-regional or inter-regional comparison could be done using any set of methods, qualitative or quantitative, and could adhere in principle to any set of commitments about the logic of inquiry. The issue which I want to highlight here is the unacknowledged work being done by the assumption of coherent regions which risks unreflectively shaping the choice of comparisons in ways that either distort or foreclose possible conclusions. The greater durability of monarchies, demonstrated through comparison with non-monarchical Arab regimes, might fade away if the comparative universe were other oil-rich rentier states. The inability of Islamists to participate in democratic elections, demonstrated through their behavior in deeply undemocratic Arab regimes, may vanish if the comparative universe expanded to include Asian, South Asian, and African cases. Gulf states such as Saudi Arabia, the UAE, and Qatar might look different if they were understood as key nodes in global finance, transit, and migration rather than as "Arab" states (Khanna, Le Renard, and Vora 2020).

Take the study of Islamist movements. There is a vast literature comparing Islamist movements across the Arab world (to which I have been pleased to contribute). Countless books and articles have examined the trajectories of Muslim Brotherhood–affiliated movements, their ideologies, their electoral performance, and their social services. The overwhelming majority of the work which seeks to go beyond a single country case study or subregional comparison (Islamists in North Africa or Islamists in the Gulf) still limits its comparative lens to the Arab countries. The costs of that limitation can be seen in some exemplary recent works which look farther: Gumuscu's (2023) comparison of Turkish Islamism with Tunisia and Egypt; Medani's (2022) examination of the role of remittances in fueling Islamist movements in Egypt, Sudan, and Somalia; Farquhar's (2016) study of the export of Saudi Islamism to Africa. Limiting the comparative universe to Arab countries makes it very difficult to isolate the real relationship between Islamism and democracy, since Arab Islamists operate within profoundly autocratic regimes where no movement, of any ideological stripe, has demonstrated democratic success. Attributing extreme violence to Islamist ideology by only looking at Middle Eastern cases, which tend to involve Islamists, risks missing the equally extreme violence of leftist, fascist, or mercenary forces in other regions. The flourishing of violent Salafi-jihadist groups across the Sahel and Africa makes it difficult to sustain assumptions about the unique susceptibility of Middle Eastern environments to such extremism. Similar problems can be seen across many domains of inquiry, from democratic transitions and authoritarianism to the prevalence and severity of civil wars.

Another dimension of the problem can best be summarized by Ella Shohat, who warned that "any serious analysis has to begin from the premise that genders, sexualities, races, classes, nations and even continents exist not as hermetically sealed entities but, rather, as part of a set of permeable, interwoven relationships" (2001: 1269). Comparative area studies can occlude critical transregional studies which capture flows and networks which cross the boundaries of regions. It is not obvious that the impact of the flow of Islamist ideas or labor remittances from the Arabian Peninsula should best be studied by comparing regions – the Middle East, South Asia, Africa – rather than by transregional analysis. Migration and refugees, ever more central to the political economy and lived culture of regional states, cannot possibly be understood without a transregional orientation. And as Israel's war on Gaza forces Palestine back onto the agenda of international organizations and into the core of politics in much of the world, from the United States to the Global South, it is not obvious that the rapidly circulating ideas about the nature of the conflict or how to respond can be usefully studied within a comparative nation-state framework.

So What to Do?

Rather than simply admire the problem, I would like to conclude with some suggestions of how to proceed with the Middle East as a region.

Celebrate area studies as the best of political science. There is no reason for so much defensiveness about area studies within the discipline. Scholarship on the region over the last several decades has, in my view, conclusively shown that it is more than possible to engage the concerns of the broader discipline through close study of Middle Eastern cases. What's more, the decade since the Arab uprisings have shown that it is not seriously possible to answer critical questions about core questions such as democratic transitions, autocratic durability, protest diffusion and dynamics, migration, civil wars, or transnational movements without reference to Middle Eastern cases.

Despite the incoherence of the regional designation, and the distorting effects described in this section, there is no denying that Middle East–focused scholars have been enormously productive in the last two decades (Lynch, Schwedler, and Yom 2022). They have overcome many of the methodological and disciplinary problems which for so long blocked development of the field, without (for the most part) sacrificing the language skills and field experience which have marked the area studies. The 1990s turn away from areas was a mistake; my call to problematize regions draws different conclusion. As Acharya (2014a) so eloquently argues, the best political science will be done by people with deep knowledge of their cases. Decades and decades of defensiveness about the viability of the area studies in general, and Middle East Studies in particular, should be abandoned for good.

Match the region to the question. Celebrating area studies does not mean accepting any particular definition of the region, however. In his 2016 history of Middle East Studies in the United States, Zachary Lockman wryly concludes that "beyond its common geographic focus, the field has an essentially institutional, pedagogical and social rather than an intellectual basis." But nonetheless, he notes, those within the field can "engage in meaningful intellectual conversation ... because despite differences of discipline and intellectual orientation they often share substantial specific and general knowledge, linguistic competence, interests and experiences." That seems like a useful starting point for picturing a way forward in the use of "the Middle East" as an organizing concept for political science. We should avoid the "congealing of contingent boundaries into reified realities" (Sinha 2013: 266) in favor of flexible definitions based on specific questions and methodological needs.

The organization of knowledge within universities inclines toward fixed sets of countries, of course, and won't easily follow such flexible notions. After all, if one is running a Middle East Studies program, one needs to know what faculty to hire, what languages to teach, and what courses to offer. But that instrumental reality does not necessarily have to translate into how we organize our research and analysis. We need to stop thinking about the Middle East as an enclosed, fixed unit of analysis and start thinking about it in terms of the particular qualities and characteristics which countries inside – and outside – of that region share which are relevant to particular questions we wish to answer. As this Element has attempted to demonstrate, many things we take for granted about the Middle East are artifacts of our quite arbitrary regional definitions. Our political science will be better when it combines deep area expertise with a much more elastic definition of the areas in question. We need to be able to theorize and research transregional connections and comparisons, seeing the world in terms of dense networks rather than discrete regions, without losing sight of the critical importance of grounded, sustained field research and local knowledge.

Decolonizing the Middle East isn't going to help ... One response to the problematic origins of the idea of the Middle East has been to rename it in the name of broader trends toward decolonization the academy (Bishara 2023; Culcasi 2023). Some of the solutions involved make excellent sense, particularly calls to more fully integrate scholars from the region and to pay more attention to scholarship and ideas emanating from the region. As Katzenstein (2001: 789) argued two decades ago, "an infusion of intellectual energy from foreign graduate students and post-docs is leading to a reinvention of traditional area studies as global networks of scholarly engagement" (789). The more that scholars "from the region" are integrated into the core of the enterprise, the more that their conceptions and reconceptualizations of what makes region will come to shape the discipline. When a Black Iranian sets out to write Iranian history, she is more likely to bring forward transregional histories of slavery and the erasure of former slaves from nationalist historiography (Baghoolizadeh 2024).

The least persuasive recommendation, though, is to replace "the Middle East" or "MENA" with SWANA (Southwest Asia and North Africa). Such a linguistic shift would have the salutary effect of rejecting the definitions associated with European colonialism, to be sure. But it would still define the region geographically in relation to a global power (in this case China) without offering any useful, unique, or defensible boundaries to the region. Adopting SWANA just follows on the long tradition detailed earlier in this Element of arbitrarily imposing definitions of the region from the outside, without solving any of the problems which that has caused.

... but subregional and transregional approaches might. The call to match region with question goes hand in hand with greater attention to subregional distinctions. The shared experience and identity of the Maghreb, the Levant, or the Gulf are orders of magnitude greater than those which bind the Middle East as a whole. Those subregions do tend to share a common history – whether with Ottoman legacies or encounters with imperialism – and similar resource endowments, degrees of stateness, institutional forms, and political culture. Green (2014) offers one of the most interesting of these subregional definitions, but there are many others on which to draw.

That said, it would be as much a mistake to reify subregions as it would be to reify the region as a whole. One of the most intellectually exciting projects of recent decades has been the rise of Indian Ocean Studies, situating the Gulf within a maritime context spanning India and the East African coast (Green 2014; Low 2022; Crouzet 2022). The Indian Ocean context allows us to see both historical and contemporary developments in genuinely new ways, rethinking the Ottoman legacy alongside British and French imperial histories and recapturing the long, deep connections between the Arabian Peninsula and the Horn of Africa. Rather than call for the designation of a new "region," Indian Ocean studies should be a model for facilitating new thinking about transregional connections and global histories. Similarly, literature connecting the Maghreb with the Sahel and French West Africa has helped to see the construction of regional borders while elucidating the political, strategic, environmental, and economic costs of arbitrary divisions.

The definition and study of the Middle East cannot not be political. This Element has raised a wide range of critical questions about the conceptualization of the Middle East as a region, highlighting the many ways in which its definition is contested. That contestation should be embraced, and studied, rather than suppressed in the name of scientific precision. I was quite taken with Schwartz's (1980) argument about Asian studies, that the question of whether Chinese values and ideas had penetrated and shaped the surrounding areas enough to create an East Asia region was a "fruitful ambiguity," an important and critically useful area for research rather than a reason to abandon area studies. Area studies should be the antidote to Orientalism, he argues, refusing to take all of the Middle East as a unified monolith precisely because of the intensity of local knowledge, language study, and lived experience. If area studies is understood as inherently cross-disciplinary, it should act as a self-corrective to the assumptions and blind spots of any single discipline. Thompson (2013) similarly mounts a persuasive defense of Southeast Asia as a region, despite all its ambiguities, in part because of the agency of those in the region seeking to organize the region along those lines. Studies of the Middle East should be expected to explicitly define and defend its borders, and to consistently consider how conclusions might change those borders be affected and different comparisons made.

The question of Israel's inclusion, and on what terms, is the elephant in the room in all discussions of the definition of the Middle East as a region, and the most openly contested politically. The war on Gaza, which began in October 2023, will only make those questions more intense. Again, this should be embraced as a question rather than ruled out of the analytical framework. Israel may always be in the Middle East, but not of it – and that should be taken as a key marker for thinking about the definition of the region rather than as a problem to be avoided. It is entirely appropriate analytically for Israel to be included in the Middle East for strategic analysis but excluded when the object of analysis is identity and regional self-definition. That triggers controversial political questions, true, but, as this Element has demonstrated, so are all definitions of region. On one vision, Israel should be included in the region on all levels, because even the rejection of its inclusion is a political act worthy of analysis and it would be virtually impossible to assess Arab identity without its Israeli Other. Furthermore, nearly a quarter of Israel's citizen population is

Palestinian Arab, a figure which grows to more than half if one takes seriously the one-state reality created by Israel's permanent occupation of the West Bank and Gaza (Barnett et al., 2023). On another, it should be excluded by virtue of its non-Arab identity and the hostility toward its project among most of the region's members. But again, these disagreements are productive rather than fatal: Israel's inclusion should be assessed across multiple dimensions, with its inclusion for the purposes of analysis not necessarily implying normalization of its presence in the region.

In Praise of Comparative and Transregional Area Studies

This Element's examination of the Middle East comes neither to bury the region nor to praise it. Excavating the intellectual and institutional history of the regional construct helps us to understand how and why its borders were drawn, as well as the stakes of those definitions and the costs of losing other definitions which might have been. It is quite possible to understand that past in all its problematic glory without abandoning the quite impressive Middle East political science research community which has been developed over the course of decades. Multiple disciplines, from history and anthropology to critical geography, are moving in the direction of transregional and cross-regional comparison. Political science should seek to emulate and elaborate those moves without prejudice to its core disciplinary strengths. Area studies, in all of its inherent interdisciplinarity, should lead the way even as it moves beyond arbitrary and misleading reifications of specific regions.

References

Aarts, P. (1999). "The Middle East: A Region without Regionalism or the End of Exceptionalism?" *Third World Quarterly* 20, 5: 911–25.

Acharya, A. (2007). "The Emerging Regional Architecture of World Politics." *World Politics* 59, 4: 629–52.

Acharya, A. (2014a). "Global International Relations (IR) and Regional Worlds: An Agenda for International Studies." *International Studies Quarterly* 58: 647–59.

Acharya, A. (2014b). "Remaking Southeast Asian Studies: Doubt, Desire, and the Promise of Comparisons." *Pacific Affairs* 87, 3: 463–83.

Adamason, F. (2016). "Spaces of Global Security: Beyond Methodological Nationalism." *Journal of Global Security Studies* 1, 1: 19–35.

Adelson, R. (1995). *London and the Invention of the Middle East: Money, Power, and War, 1902–1922*. New Haven, CT: Yale University Press.

Adler, E., F. Bicchi, B. Crawford, and R. Del Sarto, eds. (2016). *The Convergence of Civilizations: Constructing a Mediterranean Region*. Toronto: University of Toronto Press.

Ajami, F. (1978). "The End of Pan-Arabism." *Foreign Affairs* 57: 355–73.

Ajami, F. (1992). *The Arab Predicament: Arab Political Thought and Practice Since 1967*. New York: Cambridge University Press.

Ahram, A. (2011). "The Theory and Method of Comparative Area Studies." *Qualitative Research* 11, 1: 69–90.

Aidi, H., M. Lynch, and Z. Mampilly (2020). "Africa and the Middle East: Beyond Regional Divides." *POMEPS Studies* 40.

Alpher, Y. (2015). *Periphery: Israel's Search for Middle East Allies*. New York: Rowman and Littlefield.

Amour, P. O. (2017). "Israel, the Arab Spring, and the Unfolding Regional Order in the Middle East: A Strategic Assessment." *British Journal of Middle Eastern Studies* 44, 3: 293–309.

Anderson, K. (2021). *The Egyptian Labor Corps: Race, Space, and Place in the First World War*. Austin, TX: University of Texas Press..

Aras, B. and E. Yorulmazlar (2017). "Mideast Geopolitics: The Struggle for a New Order." *Middle East Policy* 24, 2: 57–69.

Aris, S. (2020). "International vs Area? The Disciplinary-Politics of Knowledge-Exchange between IR and Area Studies." *International Theory* 13: 451–82.

Ayoob, M. (1999). "From Regional System to Regional Society: Exploring Key Variables in the Construction of Regional Order." *Australian Journal of International Affairs* 53, 3: 247–60.

Baghoolizadeh, B. (2024). *The Color Black: Enslavement and Erasure in Iran.* Durham, NC: Duke University Press.

Bank, A. and J. Busse. (2021). "MENA Political Science Research a Decade after the Arab Uprisings: Facing the Facts on Tremulous Grounds." *Mediterranean Politics* 26, 5: 539–62.

Barnett, M. (1998). *Dialogues in International Politics: Negotiations in Regional Order.* New York: Columbia University Press.

Barnett, M. (1995). "Sovereignty, Nationalism and Regional Order in the Arab States System." *International Organization* 49, 3: 479–510.

Barnett, M., N. Brown, M. Lynch, and S. Telhami, eds. (2023). *The One State Reality: What Is Israel/Palestine?* Ithaca, NY: Cornell University Press.

Basedau, M. (2020). "Rethinking African Studies: Four Challenges and the Case for Comparative African Studies." *Africa Spectrum* 55, 2: 194–206.

Basedau, M. and P. Köllner. (2007). "Area Studies, Comparative Area Studies, and the Study of Politics." *Zeitschrift für Vergleichinde Politikwissenschaft* 1: 105–24.

Bates, R. (1997). "Area Studies and the Discipline: A Useful Controversy?" *PS: Political Science and Politics* 30, 2: 166–69.

Bayat, A. (2013). "Areas and Ideas." *Comparative Studies of South Asia, Africa and the Middle East* 33, 3: 260–63.

Berlin, M. S. and A. P. Syed. (2022). "The Middle East and North Africa in Middle East Scholarship: Analyzing Publication Patterns in Leading Journals, 1990–2019." *International Studies Review* 24, 3.

Bianco, C. (2024). *The Arab Gulf Monarchies after the Arab Spring.* Manchester: Manchester University Press.

Bilgin, P. (2004). "Whose Middle East? Geopolitical Inventions and Practices of Security." *International Relations* 18, 1: 25–41.

Bilgin, P. and B. Futak-Campbell. (2021). "Globalizing (the Study of) Regionalism in International Relations." In *Globalizing Regionalism in International Relations*, edited by B. Futak-Campbell, Bristol: Bristol University Press, 3–26.

Binder, L. (1958). "The Middle East as a Subordinate State System." *World Politics* 10, 3: 408–29.

Bishara, A. (2023). "Decolonizing Middle East anthropology: Toward liberations in SWANA societies." *American Ethnologist* 50, 3: 396–408.

Bonine, M. E., A. Amanat, and M. E., Gasper, eds. (2012). *Is There a Middle East? The Evolution of a Geopolitical Concept.* Palo Alto, CA: Stanford University Press.

Börzel T. and T. Risse, eds. (2016). *The Oxford Handbook of Comparative Regionalism*. New York: Oxford University Press.

Branch, A. and Z. Mampilly. (2015). *Africa Uprising: Popular Protest and Political Change*. London: Zed Books.

Brown, M. (2022). *The Seventh Member State: Algeria, France and the European Community*. Cambridge, MA: Harvard University Press.

Butt, A. I. (2013). "Anarchy and Hierarchy in International Relations: Examining South America's War-Prone Decade, 1932–41." *International Organization* 67: 575–607.

Buzan, B. and O. Waever. (2003). *Regions and Powers: The Structure of International Security*. New York: Cambridge University Press.

Byrne, J. J. (2019). *The Mecca of Revolution: Algeria, Decolonization and the Third World Order*. New York: Oxford University Press.

Cammett, M. and I. Kendall. (2022). "Political Science Scholarship on the Middle East: A View from the Journals." *PS: Political Science and Politics* 54, 3: 448–55.

Cantori, L. and S. Spiegel. (1973). "The Analysis of Regional International Politics: The Integration versus the Empirical Systems Approach." *International Organization* 27: 465–94.

Cantori, L. and S. Spiegel. (1969). "International Regions: A Comparative Approach to Five Subordinate Systems." *International Studies Quarterly* 13, 4: 361–80.

Chabal, P. (2005). "Area Studies and Comparative Politics: Africa in Context." *Afrika Spectrum* 40, 3: 471–84.

Clark, J. A. and F. Cavatorta, eds . (2018). *Political Science Research in the Middle East and North Africa*. New York: Oxford University Press.

Cooley, A. (2024). "The Uprisings of Gaza: How Geopolitical Crises Have Reshaped Academic Communities from Tahrir to Kyiv." *Political Science Quarterly* (advance publication). https://doi.org/10.1093/psquar/qqae006, 1–18.

Crouzet, G. (2022). *Inventing the Middle East: Britain and the Persian Gulf in the Age of Global Imperialism*. Montreal, CA: McGill-Queen's University Press.

Culcasi, K. (2010). "Constructing and Naturalizing the Middle East." *Geographic Review* 100, 4: 583–97.

Culcasi, K. (2023). "Decolonizing the "Middle East," *Arab World Geographer* 26, 2: 108–18.

Cumings, B. (1997). "Boundary Displacement: Area Studies and International Studies before and after the Cold War." *Bulletin of Concerned Asian Scholars* 29, 1: 6–26.

Davison, R. H. (1960). "Where Is the Middle East?" *Foreign Affairs* 38, 4: 665–75.

Dawisha, A. (2016). *Arab Nationalism in the Twentieth Century: From Triumph to Despair*. Princeton, NJ: Princeton University Press.

Debre, M. J. (2020). "The Dark Side of Regionalism: How Regional Organizations Help Authoritarian Regimes to Boost Survival." *Democratization* 28, 2: 394–413.

Del Sarto, R. A. (2020). *Borderlands: Europe and the Mediterranean Middle East*. Oxford: Oxford University Press.

Donelli, F. (2021). *Turkey in Africa: Turkey's Strategic Involvement in Sub-Saharan Africa*. London: Bloomsbury.

Eckstein, H. (1975). "A Critique of Area Studies from a West European Perspective." In *Political Science and Area Studies: Rivals or Partners*, edited by Lucian Pye. Bloomington, IN: Indiana University Press, 199–217.

Evered, K. T. (2017). "Beyond Mahan and Mackinder: Situating Geography and Critical Geopolitics in Middle East Studies." *International Journal of Middle Eastern Studies* 49, 335–39.

Fakhro, E. (2024). *The Abraham Accords*. New York: Columbia University Press.

Farquhar, M. (2016). *Circuits of Faith: Migration, Education and the Wahhabi Mission*. Palo Alto, CA: Stanford University Press.

Fawcett, L. and H. Gandois. (2010). "Regionalism in Africa and the Middle East: Implications for EU Studies." *European Integration* 32, 6: 617–36.

Fifield, R. H. (1983). "Southeast Asia as a Regional Concept." *Southeast Asian Journal of Social Science* 11, 2: 1–14.

Foliard, D. (2020). *Dislocating the Orient: British Maps and the Making of the Modern Middle East, 1854–1921*. Chicago, IL: University of Chicago Press.

Gause III, F. G. (2019). "'Hegemony' Compared: Great Britain and the United States in the Middle East." *Security Studies* 28, 3: 565–87.

Gause III, F. G. (2009). *The International Relations of the Persian Gulf*. New York: Cambridge University Press.

Gause III, F. G. (2003). "Balancing What? Threat Perception and Alliance Choice in the Gulf." *Security Studies* 13, 2: 273–305.

Gidron, Y. (2020). *Israel in Africa: Security, Migration, Interstate Politics*. London: Zed Books.

Green, N. (2014). "Rethinking the Middle East after the Oceanic Turn." *Comparative Studies of South Asia, Africa and the Middle East* 34, 2: 556–64.

Green, J. D. (1994). "The Politics of Middle East Politics." *PS: Political Science and Politics* 27, 3: 517–18.

Gumuscu, S. (2023). *Democracy or Authoritarianism: Islamist Governments in Turkey, Egypt and Tunisia*. New York: Cambridge University Press.

Hajjar, L. and S. Niva. (1997). "(Re)Made in the USA: Middle East Studies in the Global Era." *Middle East Report* 205: 2–9.

Hameiri, S. (2013). "Theorising Regions through Changes in Statehood: Rethinking the Theory and Method of Comparative Regionalism." *Review of International Studies* 39, 2: 313–35.

Hanieh, A. (2018). "Ambitions of a Global Gulf: The Arab Uprisings, Yemen, and the Saudi-Emirati Alliance." *Middle East Report* 218: 21–6.

Hannoum, A. (2022). *The Invention of the Maghreb: Between Africa and the Middle East*. New York: Cambridge University Press.

Hanson, S. (2009). "The Contribution of Area Studies." In *The Sage Handbook of Comparative Politics*, edited by T. Landman and N. Robinson, Washington, D.C.: Sage Publications, 159–74.

Hazbun, W. (2017). "The Politics of Insecurity in the Arab World: The View from Beirut." *PS: Political Science and Politics* 50, 3: 656–59.

Hegghammer, T. (2020). *The Caravan: Abdullah Azzam and the Rise of Global Jihad*. New York: Cambridge University Press.

Hettne, B. (2015). "Beyond the New Regionalism." *New Political Economy* 10, 4: 543–71.

Heydemann, S. and M. Lynch, eds. (2024). *Making Sense of the Arab State*. Ann Arbor, MI: University of Michigan Press.

Hibri, H. (2021). *Visions of Beirut: The Urban Life of Media Infrastructure*. Durham, NC: Duke University Press.

Hinnebusch, R. (2015). *The International Relations of the Middle East, 2nd ed.* Manchester: Manchester University Press.

Hintz, L. (2019). *Identity Inside and Out: National Identity Contestation and Foreign Policy in Turkey*. New York: Oxford University Press.

Hoffmann, B. (2015). "Latin America and beyond: The Case for Comparative Area Studies." *European Review of Latin American and Caribbean Studies* 100: 111–20.

Hofmeyr, I. (2012). "The Complicating Sea: The Indian Ocean as Method." *Comparative Studies in South Asia, Africa and the Middle East* 32, 3: 584–90.

Howard, M. and M. Walters. (2014). "Explaining the Unexpected: Political Science and the Surprises of 1989 and 2011." *Perspectives on Politics* 12, 2: 394–408.

Huliaris, A. and K. Magliveras. (2011). "The End of an Affair? Libya and Sub-Saharan Africa." *Journal of North African Studies* 16, 2: 167–81.

Ikenberry, G. J. and D. H. Nexon. (2019). "Hegemony Studies 3.0: The Dynamics of Hegemonic Orders." *Security Studies* 28, 3: 395–421.

Jakes, A. (2020). *Egypt's Occupation: Colonial Economism and the Crises of Capitalism*. Palo Alto, CA: Stanford University Press.

Katzenstein, P. J. (2005). *A World of Regions: Asia and Europe in the American Imperium*. Ithaca, NY: Cornell University Press.

Katzenstein, P. J. (2001). "Area and Regional Studies in the United States." *PS: Political Science and Politics* 34, 4: 789–91.

Keddie, N. R. (1973). "Is There a Middle East?" *International Journal of Middle Eastern Studies* 4, 3: 255–71.

Kerr, M. (1965). *The Arab Cold War, 1958–1964: A Study of Ideology in Politics*. London: Oxford University Press.

Khalidi, R. (1998). "The Middle East as a Framework of Analysis: Re-Mapping a Region in the Era of Globalization." *Comparative Studies of South Asia, Africa and the Middle East* 18, 1: 74–81.

Khalidi, R. (1995). "Is There a Future for Middle East Studies?" *Middle East Studies Association Bulletin* 29, 1: 1–6.

Khalil, O. F. (2016). *America's Dream Palace: Middle East Expertise and the Rise of the National Security State*. Cambridge, MA: Harvard University Press.

Khana, A., A. Le Renard, and N. Vora. (2020). *Beyond Exception: New Interpretations of the Arabian Peninsula*. Ithaca, NY: Cornell University Press.

Khosrowja, H. (2011). "A Brief History of Area Studies and International Studies." *Arab Studies Quarterly* 33, 3/4: 131–42.

Koch, N. (2017). "Geopower and Geopolitics in, of, and for the Middle East." *International Journal of Middle East Studies* 49: 315–18.

Kramer, M. (2001). *Ivory Towers on Sand: The Failure of Middle East Studies in America*. Washington, DC: Washington Institute for Near East Policy.

Kurzman, C. (2007). "Cross-Regional Approaches to Middle East Studies: Constructing and Deconstructing a Region." *MESA Bulletin* 41, 1: 24–9.

Lacroix, S. (2014). *Awakening Islam: The Politics of Religious Dissent in Saudi Arabia*. Cambridge, MA: Harvard University Press.

Lake, D. A. (2009a). "Regional Hierarchy: Authority and Local International Order." *Review of International Studies* 35: 35–58.

Lake, D. A. (2009b). *Hierarchy in International Relations*. Ithaca, NY: Cornell University Press.

Legrenzi, M. and M. Calculli (2013). *Regionalism and Regionalization in the Middle East: Options and Challenges*. New York: International Peace Institute Issue Brief.

Lewis, B. (1992). "Rethinking the Middle East." *Foreign Affairs* 71, 4: 99–119.

Lockman, Z. (2016). *Field Notes: The Making of Middle East Studies in the United States*. Palo Alto, CA: Stanford University Press.

Lockman, Z. (2003). *Contending Visions of the Middle East*. New York: Cambridge University Press.

Low, M. C. (2022). *Imperial Mecca: Ottoman Arabia and the Indian Ocean Hajj*. New York: Columbia University Press.

Lustick, I. (1997). "The Absence of Middle Eastern Great Powers: Political Backwardness in Historical Perspective." *International Organization* 51, 4: 653–83.

Lynch, M. (1999). *State Interests and Public Spheres: The International Politics of Jordan's Identity*. New York: Columbia University Press.

Lynch, M. (2022). "The End of the Middle East: How an Old Map Distorts Reality." *Foreign Affairs* 101, 2: 58–67.

Lynch, M. (2021). "Taking Stock of MENA Political Science after the Uprisings." *Mediterranean Politics* 26, 5: 682–95.

Lynch, M. (2018). "The New Arab Order: Power and Violence in Today's Middle East." *Foreign Affairs* 97, 1: 116–26.

Lynch, M. (2016). *The New Arab Wars: Anarchy and Uprising in the Middle East*. New York: Public Affairs.

Lynch, M. (2012). *The Arab Uprisings: The Unfinished Revolutions of a New Middle East*. New York: Public Affairs.

Lynch, M. (2007). *Voices of the New Arab Public: Iraq, Al-Jazeera, and Middle East Politics*. New York: Columbia University Press.

Lynch, M. and S. Mabon, eds. (2025). *Region and Order-Making in the Middle East*. Edinburgh: Edinburgh University Press.

Lynch, M., J. Schwedler, and S. Yom, eds. (2022). *The Political Science of the Middle East: Theory and Research after the Arab Uprisings*. New York: Oxford University Press.

Mabon, S. (2020). *Houses Built on Sand: Violence, Sectarianism and Revolution in the Middle East*. Manchester: Manchester University Press.

Mabon, S. and R. Mason, eds. (2022). *The Gulf States and the Horn of Africa*. Manchester: Manchester University Press.

Malley, R. (1996). *The Call From Algeria: Third Worldism, Revolution, and the Turn to Islam*. Berkeley: University of California Press.

Mansfield, E. D. and E. Solingen. (2010). "Regionalism." *Annual Reviews of Political Science* 13, 145–63.

Martz, J. (1971). "Political Science and Latin American Studies: A Discipline in Search of a Region." *Latin American Research Review* 6, 1: 73–99.

Mathews, N. (2024). *Zanzibar Was a Country: Exile and Citizenship between East Africa and the Gulf*. Berkeley, CA: University of California Press.

Mattern, J. B. and A. Zarakol. (2016). "Hierarchies in World Politics." *International Organization* 70: 623–54.

Matthiesen, T. (2023). *The Caliph and the Imam*. New York: Oxford University Press.

Mazrui, A. (1974). "Black Africa and the Arabs." *Foreign Affairs* 53: 725–42.

McConnaughy, M., P. Musgrave, and D. Nexon. (2018). "Beyond Anarchy: Logics of Political Organization, Hierarchy and International Structure." *International Theory* 10, 2: 181–218.

Medani, K. (2022). *Black Markets and Militants*. New York: Cambridge University Press.

Mikdashi, M. (2023). "Ethnography, Cacophany, and Lebanon as a Zone of Prestige in the Anthropology of the Middle East." *American Ethnologist* 50, 206–207.

"Mission Statement," (2013). *Comparative Studies of South Asia, Africa and the Middle East* 33 (2), 135–36.

Mitchell, T. (2003). "The Middle East in the Past and Future of Social Science." In *The Politics of Knowledge: Area Studies and Disciplines*, edited by D. Szanton. Berkeley, CA: University of California Press, 74–118.

Mitzen, J. (2006). "Ontological Security in World Politics: State Identity and the Security Dilemma." *European Journal of International Relations* 12, 3: 341–70.

Monier, E. (2014). "The Arabness of Middle Eastern Regionalism: The Arab Spring and Competition for Discursive Hegemony between Egypt, Iran and Turkey." *Contemporary Politics* 20, 4: 421–34.

Neep, D. (2012). *Occupying Syria under the French Mandate: Insurgency, Space, and State Formation*. New York: Cambridge University Press.

Noble, P. (1991). "The Arab System: Pressures, Constraints, and Opportunities." In *The Foreign Policies of Arab States*, edited by B. Korany and A. H. Dessouki. Boulder, CO: Westview Press, 49–102.

O'Malley, A. (2021). "A Global Perspective on Pan Movements: Regional Anomalies or Abnormal Regions?" In *Globalizing Regionalism in International Relations*, edited by B. Futak-Campbell. Bristol: Bristol University Press, 27–47.

Payne, A. (1998). "The New Political Economy of Area Studies." *Millennium* 27, 2: 253–73.

Pepinsky, Thomas J. (2023). Southeast Asia and *World Politics*. 75th Anniversary Issue. *World Politics*. https://dx.doi.org/10.1353/wp.0.a915396.

Prewitt, K. (1996)." Presidential Items." *Items* 50, 1: 15–18.

Rafael, V. (1994). "The Cultures of Area Studies." *Social Text* 41: 91–111.

Riggirozi, P. (2012). "Region, Regionness and Regionalism in Latin America: Towards a New Synthesis." *New Political Economy* 17, 4: 421–43.

Russett, B. (1967). *International Regions and the International System.* Chicago: University of Chicago Press.

Ryan, C. (2009). *Inter-Arab Alliances: Regime Security and Jordanian Foreign Policy.* Gainesville, FL: University of Florida Press.

Sadowski, Y. (1993). "The New Orientalism and the Democracy Debate." *Middle East Report* 183: 14–21, 40.

Said, E. (1979). *Orientalism.* New York: Vintage.

Said, E. (1981). *Covering Islam: How the Media and the Experts Determine How We See the Rest of the World.* New York: Vintage.

Salloukh, B. (2018). "A New Grand Bargain for the Middle East: The Search for a new Consociational and Geopolitical Order." *The Century Foundation* (February 21).

Santini, R. H. (2017). "A New Regional Cold War in the Middle East and North Africa: Regional Security Complex Theory Revisited." *International Spectator* 52, 4: 93–111.

Schwartz, B. (1980). "Area Studies as a Critical Discipline." *The Journal of Asian Studies* 40, 1: 15–25.

Sela, A. (1998). *The Decline of the Arab-Israeli Conflict: Middle East Politics and the Quest for Regional Order.* Albany, NY: State University of New York Press.

Shamy, S. and C. Miller-Idriss, eds. (2016). *Middle East Studies for a New Millennium.* New York: New York University Press.

Shehata, S., ed. (2022). *The Struggle to Reshape the Middle East in the 21st Century.* Edinburgh: Edinburgh University Press.

Shohat, E. (2002). "Area Studies, Gender Studies, and the Cartographies of Knowledge." *Social Text* 20, 3: 67–78.

Shohat, E. (2001). "Area Studies, Transnationalism, and the Feminist Production of Knowledge." *Signs* 26, 4: 1269–72.

Sinha, M. (2013). "Is 'Region' Still Good to Think?" *Comparative Studies of South Asia, Africa and the Middle East* 33, 3: 264–67.

Smith, B. and D. Waldner. (2021). *Rethinking the Resource Curse.* New York: Cambridge University Press.

Solingen, E. (2007). "Pax Asiatica vs Bella Levantina: The Foundations of War and Peace in East Asia and the Middle East." *American Political Science Review* 101, 4: 757–80.

Sørli, M. E., N. P. Gleditsch, and H. Strand. (2005). "Why Is There So Much Conflict in the Middle East?" *Journal of Conflict Resolution* 49, 1: 49–65.

Stein, E. (2021). *International Relations in the Middle East*. New York: Cambridge University Press.

Stetter, S. (2008). *World Society and the Middle East: Reconstructions in Regional Politics*. New York: Palgrave Macmillan.

Takriti, A. R. (2013). *Monsoon Revolution: Republicans, Sultans and Empires in Oman, 1965–76*. New York: Oxford University Press.

Tessler, M., J. Nachtwey, and A. Banda, eds. (1999). *Area Studies and Social Science: Strategies for Understanding Middle East Politics*. Bloomington, IN: Indiana University Press.

Teti, A. (2007). "Bridging the Gap: IR, Middle East Studies, and the Disciplinary Problem of the Area Studies Controversy." *European Journal of International Relations* 13, 1: 117–45.

Teti, A. and P. Abbott. (2023). "Scholarship on the Middle East in Political Science and International Relations: A Reassessment." *PS: Political Science and Politics* 56, 2: 259–64.

Thompson, E. C. (2013). "In Defence of Southeast Asia: A Case for Methodological Regionalism." *TraNS: Trans-regional and -National Studies of Southeast Asia* 1, 2: 281–302.

Thompson, W. R. (1981). "Delineating Regional Subsystems: Visit Networks and the Middle Eastern Case." *International Journal of Middle East Studies* 13: 213–35.

Thompson, W. R. (1973). "The Regional Subsystem: A Conceptual Explication and a Propositional Inventory." *International Studies Quarterly* 17, 1: 89–117.

Valbjørn, M. (2016). "The Middle East and North Africa." In *The Oxford Handbook of Comparative Regionalism*, edited by T. Borzel and T. Risse. New York: Oxford University Press. 249–270.

Valbjørn, M. (2003). "The Meeting of the Twain: Bridging the Gap between International Relations and Middle East Studies." *Cooperation and Conflict* 38, 2: 163–73.

Watkins, J. (2013). "The New Mediterranean Studies: A Mediator between Area Studies and Global Studies." *Mediterranean Studies* 21: 149–54.

Wedeen, L. (2016). "Scientific Knowledge, Liberalism and Empire: American Political Science in the Modern Middle East." In *Area Studies for a New Millennium*, edited by S. Shamy and C. Miller-Idriss. New York: New York University Press. 31–81.

Willis, J. (2009). "Making Yemen India: Rewriting the Boundaries of Imperial Arabia." *International Journal of Middle East Studies* 41, 1: 23–38.

Wyrtzen, J. (2022). *Worldmaking in the Long Great War: How Local and Colonial Struggles Shaped the Modern Middle East*. New York: Columbia University Press.

Zeleza, P. T. (1997). "The Perpetual Solitudes and Crises of African Studies in the United States." *Africa Today* 44, 2: 193–210.

Cambridge Elements

Middle East Politics

David B. Roberts
King's College London

David B. Roberts is Reader in International Security and Middle East Studies at King's College London. He is also the Head of Professional Education and Enterprise in the King's Institute for Applied Security Studies (KIASS) and leads a twin-track Arabic and English Master of Research (MRes) program in the School of Security Studies

Louise Fawcett
University of Oxford

Louise Fawcett is Professor of International Relations and Senior Research Fellow at the Department of Politics and International Relations, and Fellow of St Catherine's College, University of Oxford. She is a co-director of the Oxford Martin School program, "Changing Global Order" (https://www.politics.ox.ac.uk/project/oxford-martin-programme-changing -global-order).

Mohammed Abdel-Haq
King's College London

Dr. Mohammed Abdel-Haq is Professor in Banking and the Director of the Centre for Islamic Finance, the Director of the Centre for Opposition Studies and Assistant Vice Chancellor for Postgraduate Development at the University of Bolton. He is also the Principal of Hume Institute for Postgraduate Studies, Lausanne, Switzerland; Affiliate Professor, Kings College London and an Associate at London School of Economics – IDEAS.

About the Series

Elements in Middle East Politics provides a platform for scholars to explore subjects of contemporary resonance in relation to the broader Middle East at a time when this most pivotal of regions faces profound flux. Studies focus on thematic and country focused analyses, as well ideas and approaches that seek to decolonize knowledge and highlight new disciplinary trends.

Cambridge Elements ≡

Middle East Politics

Elements in the Series

What is the Middle East? The Theory and Practice of Regions
Marc Lynch

A full series listing is available at: www.cambridge.org/EMEP